Arthur the Dragon King

Also by Howard Reid

In Search of the Immortals

Arthur
the Dragon King

The Barbaric Roots of Britain's
Greatest Legend

Howard Reid

HEADLINE

First published in 2001
by HEADLINE BOOK PUBLISHING

10 9 8 7 6 5 4 3 2 1

British Library Cataloguing in Publication Data

Reid, Howard
Arther, the dragon king
1.Arthur, King 2.Kings and rulers – Folklore
3.Arthurian romances
I.Title
398.2'2

ISBN 0 7472 7557 2 (hardback)
ISBN 0 7472 7558 0 (trade paperback)

Typeset by Letterpart Ltd
Reigate, Surrey

Printed and bound in Great Britain by
Mackays of Chatham plc, Chatham, Kent

HEADLINE BOOK PUBLISHING
A division of Hodder Headline
338 Euston Road
London NW1 3BH

www.headline.co.uk
www.hodderheadline.com

Contents

Preface

In the 1520s the Holy Roman Emperor Maximilian I decided to build a mausoleum to immortalize his dynasty in the city of Innsbruck. He commissioned a series of twenty-eight cast-bronze statues, all over seven feet tall – of himself, his family and his imperial antecedents. These figures now form two columns down each side of the church. At the centre of one row is the statue of the man who Maximilian considered to be the founder of the Hapsburg dynasty – a magnificent armour-clad figure bearing a mighty sword and a simple title: Arthur. Around his neck is draped an elaborate chain of office composed entirely of writhing, seething dragons.

Why should the most powerful man in early Renaissance Europe choose to nominate an obscure, semi-legendary British king as the well-spring of his dynasty, and why should he festoon his chosen patriarch in wreaths of dragons?

Around 500 BC, fierce nomadic warriors buried their dead leaders under massive funerary mounds at the very end of the known world, in the wild mountains of south-west Siberia. Their tombs contained elaborate votive offerings, superb works of art wrought in gold, wood, bronze and fabrics. Ancient carpets, felt wall-hangings, jewellery, weapons and armour are adorned with images of a paragon of magical animal spirit-beings. Centaurs, griffins, sphinxes and dragons abound. Even the mummified bodies of their dead are adorned with superb tattoos of the same magical beasts.

Around AD 700, Irish Celtic monks set about writing and illuminating one of the greatest medieval manuscripts of all time: the Book of Kells. *Throughout, the manuscript is adorned with magical animal spirit-beings which are near-identical to the fabulous beasts of the Siberian tombs.*

Is this mere coincidence, or could there be threads of human communication, of divine inspiration which have woven their way across 3000 miles of space and 1000 years of time, and could the soul of Arthur somehow be entangled in this fantastical web?

Still, today, the British army call their cavalrymen 'dragoons', a name derived from the word dragon, its usage traceable to the Roman occupation of Britain, Arthur's days.

Acknowledgements

This is a work of synthesis, collecting strands of thought from many diverse sources and weaving them together to produce my version of what has happened. As is so often the case when dealing with relatively obscure source material, there tends to be only one or two real experts in many of the special areas I have wanted to find out about. Because I have chosen not to use footnotes as 'credits', I want to acknowledge here the main sources of information which have moulded my thought lines.

The idea of a 'Sarmatian connection' with the stories of king Arthur dates back at least as early as the eleventh century AD, although it was only given serious scholarly consideration in the nineteenth century. In recent years the cause has been championed by two American scholars, C. Scott Littleton and Linda A. Malcor. I was introduced to their work by Victor Mair while we were working with the nomadic population in Xinjiang province, western China, in 1996. Their ideas are of key importance and reveal many of the historical and symbolic links between the worlds of central Asia and ancient Britain. I am, therefore, greatly indebted to their work, which is summarized in their jointly authored book *From Scythia to Camelot*. I should, however, mention that both their methods and the conclusions they reach are quite different from my own.

A vast amount of material of very variable quality has poured forth over the centuries about king Arthur. Among the more recent offerings, John Morris's epic, *The Age of Arthur*, is the most comprehensive and reliable study of the area, and *King Arthur in Legend and History*, edited by Richard White, contains virtually all the key sources in conveniently reduced (although still massive) form. John Darrah's book, *Paganism in Arthurian Romance,* gave me a great deal of help in pinning down the symbolic content of the Arthurian canon, although his inference that all Arthurian paganism is derived from pre-Christian Celtic tradition is at odds with my own findings.

Miranda Green is our most outstanding scholar of the ancient Celtic world, and her work has certainly given me the most vivid picture of the lifestyles, customs and beliefs of those people. The Roman Empire, and its views of the peoples of Britain and the barbarian cavalry from the steppes, are fortunately available to us from first-hand sources – Caesar, Tacitus, Cassius Dio and Ammianus Marcellinus are all key sources. In a similar vein, Herodotus's accounts of early Scythian culture and history are, in my view, some of the most invaluable documents ever set down.

The great Russian archaeologist, Sergei Rudenko, has provided us with both the material and the interpretation of the archaeological facts which corroborate Herodotus and give us extraordinary insights into the ancient steppe civilization of the Scythians. More recent work in Russia by the German archaeologist, Renate Rolle, provides yet more insight into these fascinating people, summarized in her book *The World of the Scythians*.

The Sarmatians is a monograph by the Polish-British scholar Tadeuz Sulimirski. Published in 1970, it has yet to be surpassed for its detailed treatment of the people who may well have brought many of the elements of the Arthurian legends to British shores in the first place. Three years after Sulimirski's book was published, an American scholar, Bernard Bachrach, published *A History of the Alans in the West*, and this too has remained the definitive source on the subject. In addition, one wide-ranging work, which covers most of the period and many of the peoples I investigate, is *The Oxford Illustrated Prehistory of Europe*, edited by Barry Cunliffe. It has been an enormous help in sorting out the complex and relatively obscure history covered in this book. At a more accessible level, Neil Ascherson's book, *Black Sea*, is not only a wonderful tale of travel and adventure, it is also crammed full of fascinating information pertaining to the apposite history of the region where the Cimmerians, Scythians, Sarmatians and finally the Huns and Alans washed up on the shores of Europe.

On a more personal level, Victor Mair has been wonderfully encouraging and supportive of this project from its inception, and has provided inspirational guidance and insights. Marsha Levine has been very kind and helpful in improving my understanding of the origins of horsemanship and early life on the steppes in general. Tim Taylor, whose contributions to Barry Cunliffe's book and to the *Cambridge Ancient History* and the *Dictionary of Art* provide the best material on the aesthetics and history of the steppe warriors, has been most generous with his time and understanding of the peoples and period in question.

Although I am greatly indebted to all the people mentioned above for their scholarly contributions to my subject matter, I remain responsible for the opinions expressed in this book, and for any errors of fact or judgement it may contain.

My two book researchers, Pippa Dennis and Kate Solomon, have been brilliant at tracking down many of the obscure sources I needed to consult and for visiting several of the locations with me. My editor, Douglas ('Dark Water') Young has been, as always, wonderfully supportive and courteous, the very flower of twenty-first-century chivalry, while my agent, Mark Lucas, has been surprisingly jovial and relatively uncritical by his standards. (Whether this is a good sign or bad, I am not sure.) My copy editor, Barbara Nash, has as always done a superb job with the manuscript and remains a delight to work with.

Finally, I thank my wife Val and my three daughters, Amie, Leila and Maya for all their support as I both researched and wrote this book, mostly from my study at home.

CHAPTER ONE

The Mighty Shadow

THE TALES OF KING ARTHUR AND HIS KNIGHTS OF THE ROUND TABLE ARE among the most popular and enduring legends in the world. Most English-speaking people have known them since they were small children: they mark a beginning – the birth of a nation, the bedrock of the British national character. Before Arthur, the British were mere tribals, lurking in the murky shadows of prehistory. After him, they were a people. Arthur is an archetypal hero – a magical warrior king who lived, loved and died as the soul of romantic tragedy. His tales have inspired some of the greatest heroic literature and art of the last millennium, from their inception in AD 1136 with Geoffrey of Monmouth's *The History of the Kings of Britain* to their intergalactic rebirth 840 years later in George Lucas's *Star Wars*.

I first learnt the stories of Arthur as a child. By the time I was seven years old, I certainly reckoned I knew this piece of our national 'history'. I, my brother and our gang only needed a couple of nails to hammer two bits of wood together then sharpen one end, and there was our Excalibur. We would sometimes thrust it into the soft walls of a small chalk pit at the end of our garden then withdraw it, triumphantly freeing the sword from the stone. We even knew to take the sword and touch the shoulders of a kneeling gang member, bidding him arise as 'Sir Galahad' or 'Sir Lancelot'.

During the long wintry evenings my father would sometimes read to us from *Our Island Story,* by H.E. Marshall, and my dreams would prickle with misty visions of the dying king, his magical barge and the hand of the Lady of the Lake wielding Excalibur above the rippling waters of Avalon. The shadowy figure of the Druid Merlin conjured up not just magic swords but the cloud-capped towers of Camelot, the great round table, wondrous knights – such as Lancelot, Galahad and Gawain – in shining armour, and the glistening golden Holy Grail. I knew that like them one day I too would set off on epic quests, and I certainly planned to rescue damsels in distress and save the motherland from the ravages of heathen Saxon invaders.

It scarcely crossed my mind then that all this gloriously fun stuff was anything other than historical truth with which we were encouraged to play. At that age it didn't matter anyway. The tales of Arthur and his knights gave me and my friends the keys to another world – the glorious past. They let us into a Golden Age, peopled by heroes and monsters, where acts of heroism or dastardly treachery were the order of the day.

I loved the tales and tried to memorize them. I do not remember any specific beginning, but the first events I recall seemed to focus around Merlin. King Uther Pendragon had built a castle, but it kept falling down. His court magicians advised him that he should sacrifice a child to stabilize the land and the boy Merlin was chosen. He said he could solve the mystery without losing his life. He ordered the royal masons to dig a pit, and there he eventually uncovered two battling dragons, one white, representing the Saxons, the other red, representing the Britons. Eventually the white dragon drove out the red one, a bad omen that signalled the defeat of the Britons (red dragon) by the Saxons (white dragon).

Having revealed his powers of sorcery, Merlin was adopted by Uther Pendragon, and some time later the king demanded a great favour of him. The king had fallen in love with the wife of the Duke of Cornwall and somehow contrived to separate the couple. Laying siege to the duke, Uther Pendragon eventually broke through the castle's defences and killed him. That evening Uther begged Merlin to transform him into the likeness of the duke. Merlin agreed to do this, but on one condition. The child born of this deception should be given to Merlin to rear until he reached manhood. This duly agreed, Uther rode into Tintagel, the castle where the duchess was sheltering. She bade the likeness of her husband enter and the disguised Uther had his way with her, conceiving a son in her womb. After receiving confirmation of her husband's death and of the trick which had deceived her, she allowed Uther Pendragon to marry her, thus becoming queen.

When Arthur was born he was duly assigned to Merlin the Druid to rear him in secrecy, away from the court. Although we are not told it, I have always assumed that Arthur must have grown up in the cocoon of Merlin's magic, nurtured and strengthened by it, perhaps even initiated into some of its secrets. Evidently he did not know his true identity at that time.

The years passed, and, following the practice of the times, Arthur was apprenticed as groom to a great knight, so that he might learn to fight. At the same time he would be taught how to conduct himself honourably, according to the code of chivalry. While Arthur was still in training, the great knight was summoned to the royal court, as king Uther Pendragon had died, apparently leaving no heir. Arthur came along as part of the great knight's retinue.

The shadowy Merlin had reappeared after the king's death and planted a sword firmly in a stone, declaring that he who could draw the sword from the stone should succeed to the throne.

All the minor kings and great barons and knights tried their luck, but none succeeded until Arthur chanced upon the sword when it was unattended. Effortlessly freeing it from the stone, he took the prize to the other knights who were so amazed that they forced the youth to put the sword back and pull it out again. This done, they reluctantly accepted Arthur as the successor to the high kingship.

Not all the nobles accepted Arthur, however, and civil war soon erupted, with several of the minor British kings joining forces to oppose the youthful high king. After a close-fought series of battles Arthur finally held sway, driving out the rebel nobles and minor kings and offering his hand in friendship to those who would swear loyalty to him.

Throughout the great struggle, Arthur was armed with a magic sword called Excalibur, which Merlin arranged for him, although it was the gift of the Lady of the Lake, a potent goddess who lived in an underwater world. So, at that time, Arthur had two magic swords – the one he pulled from the stone and Excalibur.

Arthur and his men of course travelled and fought on horseback, at least until they were unsaddled, when combat would continue on foot until a fellow knight, groom or squire would rescue the heavily armoured warrior and help him to remount. Common people – serfs and the like – made up the infantry; men of status rode to war as cavalry. Arthur himself led his troops under his battle standard, the golden dragon. Although most of the battles were all-out engagements, there were also many opportunities for single combat, where Arthur or one of his closest allies took on and eventually dispatched particular rebel nobles or kings, sometimes taking their heads and spiking them on their lances as gestures of contempt.

Once his kingdom was secure, Arthur set about the most pressing task of his times, the halting of the Saxon invasions from across the North Sea, from what is now Holland and Germany. The Saxons were formidable enemies who had already occupied much of eastern England. Pretending to sue for peace, they had made a great slaughter of the British nobles at a feast some years before Arthur came to power. They were certainly treacherous, and the only way to deal with them was by force of arms. A series of battles ensued, culminating in a great victory at Mount Badon (usually held to be somewhere near Bath), where Arthur's cavalry decidedly beat the Saxons, pushing them back to the easternmost margins of his kingdom.

Arthur then fell in love with the fairest woman in the land, Guinevere, queen of the 'Summer Country' (which some say is the county of Somerset, while others maintain Cornwall). Leading her to Camelot, his beautiful castle, they set up court ushering in a Golden Age. Pennants fluttered from the sheer stone walls while knights constantly crossed the drawbridge over the moat, on their way to and from epic quests.

Tourneys (ritual mock fights where the object was to defeat but not kill one's opponent) kept the knights fit and in good fighting trim, as well as providing grounds for the winning of favours from the ladies. The strongest of the knights became Arthur's champions and fought for him and Guinevere at the tourneys. This in turn engendered competition among the knights for Arthur's favour which was most clearly demonstrated in Camelot's Great Hall, where knights would vie with each other for the right to sit next to, or at least close to the king. When this rivalry reached fever pitch, with fights threatened at almost every meal, Arthur ordained that a round table should be built so that his knights could not be ranked by their distance from him.

With such an equitable and chivalrous order, Camelot and the court of king Arthur became famous throughout Europe, attracting many of Europe's finest knights to it. Among these came the bravest, boldest, finest knight in the world – Lancelot. A Breton, Lancelot was the undisputed champion of all champions, and Arthur took him straight to his heart, appointing him to serve as champion to queen Guinevere, the most beautiful woman in the world. Like Arthur, Lancelot was also armed with a magic sword which he had received from the Lady of the Lake, who had reared him and taught him to bear arms in her underwater world. This made him almost Arthur's equal. Alas, Guinevere also took Lancelot to her heart – and to her bosom.

So the worm entered the apple and the Golden Age began to wane.

But before the Fall, Arthur set his knights on the ultimate epic quest. It was said that in the centuries after Christ's death the Holy Grail – the chalice used by Christ at the last supper which was also used to collect his blood either at the crucifixion or the deposition of Christ's body – had disappeared. According to tradition the Holy Grail had been brought to England by Joseph of Arimathea, the first Christian missionary to Britain, and then it had vanished.

The quest of the Holy Grail was an individual undertaking, testing each of Arthur's finest knights to the ultimate. Only a knight of absolute purity of body, heart and mind could succeed. The price of failure was the risk of death from a fiery lance hurled at the loser. Lancelot failed the quest because his affair with Guinevere had sullied him. Percival, Gawain, Bors and many others also failed. In the end it was Galahad, Lancelot's son, who achieved the Grail, but not before it had broken the spirits of many of the finest knights of the round table.

Although each knight had his own adventures which were recounted when they returned to Arthur's court, their experiences were often quite similar. Typically, as a knight travelled across the wilderness he would come to a pool, lake or stream amid a grove of trees. There he would pause for a while. Then he would meet a beautiful damsel, sometimes resting in the shade of the trees, sometimes in her own tent. The knight was naturally attracted to the girl, who flirted with him. Then suddenly a fierce, often black-clad knight appeared, the guardian of the holy grove and the girl's champion, or perhaps her captor. The black knight challenged the newcomer to a fight to the death, first on horseback with lances, then, when one or both parties were forced from their horses, on the ground.

Invariably the heroic newcomer defeated the guardian, and in many cases took his head. The damsel, freed from her black knight, sometimes requested his head, to use his blood for magical healing. Then the victorious knight would go on his way in pursuit of his greater quest.

During the years of the Grail Quest, Arthur stayed rather in the background, but as the affair between Lancelot and Guinevere became more and more publicly visible, Arthur was eventually forced to act, driving Lancelot out of England back to his native France. But in the course of his expulsion, Lancelot killed Gawain's brother. By this time Gawain was Arthur's champion and he eventually persuaded Arthur to pursue Lancelot in France. Before leaving, Arthur appointed his illegitimate son Mordred and Guinevere as custodians of the kingdom. (Mordred was the product of Arthur's incestuous relationship with his sorceress sister Morgan Le

Fay, who, having cast a spell over her brother, forced him to seduce her.)

The appointment of the bastard Mordred as regent was Arthur's greatest, and most fatal mistake. For while Arthur was fighting in France, Mordred seized the throne and forced himself upon his step-mother Guinevere.

When news of the deceit reached Arthur he hurried back to England, only to be met by an army raised against him by Mordred. A pitched battle ensued and there was massive slaughter. At the end it appeared that only Arthur and Mordred stood, facing one another. Mordred delivered a mighty blow to his father's head, cutting through his helmet and piercing his skull. Inflamed with rage by the blow, Arthur turned on Mordred and cut him down with Excalibur. Mordred fell dead and the injured Arthur was carried from the field on his shield by the few remaining survivors.

Mortally wounded, the great king was taken to the shores of a lake which contained the Isle of Avalon (some say this was Glastonbury Tor), where they laid him down to rest. Here he instructed his liegeman Bedevere to take the magic sword Excalibur, cast it into the lake, then return and tell him what he had seen. Bedevere went down to the waterside but could not bring himself to throw such a fine, wondrous and beautiful weapon into the water. Returning to Arthur, the king asked him what he had seen. Bedevere reported nothing untoward. Arthur knew he was lying and ordered Bedevere to return to the lake and cast the sword in. Bedevere went once more to the lakeside, but again could not bear to part with the wondrous sword. Again Arthur knew he was lying and warned Bedevere that his life was fast ebbing away, so the sword must be disposed of as he ordered.

Returning once more to the water, Bedevere took up the sword, wrapped its strappings round the pommel, and hurled the weapon far out over the water. As it fell to the surface a hand and arm appeared from the water, caught the sword, brandished it three times in the air, then vanished with the sword below the surface.

Arthur, content with Bedevere's description of the return of the sword to the Lady of the Lake, bade Bedevere carry him to the water's side, where a beautiful barge with many fair ladies aboard awaited him. Three queens took charge of the dying king, one of them placing his head in her lap as the barge slipped away from the land. Once Arthur was out of view Bedevere wept for his lost king, and took off to the forest.

It is said, though, that king Arthur never really died, and that one day when his country really needs him he will return, the 'Once and Future King'.

This is of course the accepted version of the Arthurian legends, the version handed down to me as a child. It is a wonderful tale, with all its melodrama, passion, honour, skulduggery and barely veiled lustiness. But is all, or *any*, of it true? Did Arthur *really* exist? Because it is such a seminal tale, so critical in our definition of who the British really are, these questions need to be addressed.

For almost as long as his stories have been told, people have sought to identify the man behind the myth. But Arthur – and Merlin, Guinevere, Lancelot and Camelot, and even the Holy Grail – seem to have largely eluded the annals of history. Most scholars have traced the Arthurian tales to the mists of our Celtic past, around the time of the collapse of the Roman Empire at the turn of the fifth and sixth centuries AD. Yet there is not a single written mention of him at the time he is supposed to have reigned, nor for several centuries beyond that date. The first even vaguely reliable mention comes in the ninth century from an ecclesiastical chronicler, who calls him not a king but a war leader. The same source also mentions him as a mythical figure who is said to have killed his son in battle, and whose hunting dog left an imprint of its foot on a prominent rock.

Many of the early references to Arthur are written recordings of oral traditions — ballads, praise songs or fragments of epic poetry. Again these were written down several centuries after the time Arthur may have lived, but they do tell us that even in those early days Arthur was becoming the stuff of myth and legend. The picture is still very hazy — of a mighty king or war leader, sometimes even a cruel tyrant, victorious in many battles, although quite where and against whom he fought is far from clear. The 'mighty shadow' slips through our fingers again.

There are two possible reasons why the evidence for a historical Arthur's existence is so thin. First, he may not have existed at all; second, the period when he is said to have lived was a time of colossal turbulence, not just in Britain but all over Europe and even further to the east, as far as the heart of Asia. There was little time for the art of writing and much opportunity for the destruction of any manuscripts which were produced. Arthur's time falls conveniently right in the middle of the biggest black hole in our recorded history.

Anarchy reigned after the Roman withdrawal from Britain at the beginning of the fifth century AD. The native, Celtic-speaking Britons were harried from the north by the Picts and Caledonii, from the west by the Irish (known then, confusingly, as the Scotii) and from the east by invading Angles, Saxons and Jutes. In continental Europe the Roman Empire buckled under successive waves of invasion. The invaders were branded 'barbarians' by the Romans, following the Greek name for those who spoke 'babbled' languages, and the label stuck. Much of the history of the Roman Empire revolved around their continual efforts to keep the 'barbarians' in check, a struggle they eventually lost. Ever since, the peoples of 'civilized' Europe have lived in fear of the demonized hordes from the East.

These huge upheavals destroyed both the Roman state and its cultural heritage. Classical ideals of 'civilized' behaviour perished alongside the Roman social order as the chaos of the Dark Ages enveloped Europe. Yet relatively quickly a new order and ideology emerged from the gloom. Its ethical code came to be known as chivalry, the cult of the horse. Two key elements lay at the core of this code of honour: martial skills on horseback determined the valour and worth of the individual, ideally in single combat, and women were elevated to almost divine status. Courtly love admonished followers of the chivalric code to treat the pursuit of a woman's favour as the pinnacle of the warrior quest.

Eventually these notions would find their most perfect expression in the medieval tales of king Arthur, the knights of the round table, the quest for the Holy Grail and ultimately, the great king's death. To deepen the mystery of the chivalric code, a whole set of magical symbols embroidered the fabric of the doctrine. Fearsome beasts, both real and imaginary – lions, bears, eagles, boar, griffins, unicorns, dragons – were adopted by individuals, clans and dynasties as symbols of their power, paving the way for the rise of heraldry throughout the noble houses of medieval Europe.

In a similar vein, the Arthurian legends are shot through with hundreds of episodes which contain mystical, supernatural events and beings. These are routinely assigned to the 'pagan' culture of the Celto-Britons, but not all of them can be found there. In all sorts of ways, then, the simple equation that the Arthurian world was a direct descendant of early Celtic Britain does not add up.

So where had this 'new' ideology come from? It was certainly not a direct legacy from Rome – the Romans treated women as second-class citizens at best and had no developed ethos relating to horsemanship. Beyond the confines of the Coliseum they showed little interest in single combat and relied heavily on their superior organizational and logistical skills in marshalling their infantry in major military confrontations. Heroism was a highly manipulated political art in ancient Rome, with emperors engineering military victories to glorify themselves in triumphal parades a long way from the cold steel of the battlefield. Although the imperial eagle stood at the head of their legions, the Romans paid scant attention to the mystical powers of magical beings. So it is impossible to discern the rise of chivalry in the ashes of the Roman Empire.

This leaves conventional wisdom, which attributes the rise of the new order to the revival of the traditional pre-Roman worlds of the Celtic peoples, veneered with a shallow coating of the newly arrived ideology of Christianity. This is the usual starting-point when scholars seek either to trace the 'real' Arthur in the scant historical and archaeological records, or to search for his identity in the much later written works which immortalized him in the eleventh to fifteenth centuries.

There are obviously good reasons to accept this perspective. If Arthur did indeed live in fifth- to sixth-century Britain then he would certainly have been a Celtic-speaking Briton. Whether king or war leader (most current scholarship favours the latter), as a member of the post-Roman nobility he would certainly have been influenced by Rome's domination of his country just a few generations before his birth. But the little evidence we have makes it quite clear that post-Roman Britain was not dominated by heavily armed knights on horseback sallying forth from their castles to defend the honour of their ladies. Arthur's story is certainly set in a post-Roman Celto-British world, and my first step in trying to disentangle this great enigma will be to take a close look at traditional ancient British culture. But right from the start we will see that the Arthurian tales have never been an accurate reflection of fifth- to sixth-century Britain. They simply contain too many elements which cannot be traced to those times.

Where should we search, then, for the missing elements? To the west, beyond Ireland, there is only the ocean for 3000 miles; to the north-east is Scandinavia, but the people of these icy lands would not play a significant role in British history until the Danish and Viking invasions, centuries after Arthur's days; to the east, mainland Europe was just emerging from turmoil at the end of the fifth century. The fermenters of this maelstrom originated largely in north-eastern Europe but they had been joined by others – mounted warriors from central Asia, bearing great hissing silken dragons as their battle standards.

From the Roman perspective, these people were barbarians – both inferior and a threat to the 'civilized' world. The same hazy image prevails today. We think of the early steppe nomads – and later the mighty Mongol army of Genghis Khan – as the 'Storm from the East', invading barbarian hordes bent on looting, pillage, rape and the destruction of our 'civilized' world. We see them as savage, ruthless destroyers, the purveyors of chaos and anarchy.

Archaeological and historical records from both Greece and China flatly contradict this characterization. From the time they first took to riding horses around 1000 BC, the nomad peoples of central Asia rapidly developed highly sophisticated cultures. They produced wondrous works of art in gold, silk, bronze and iron, and grew into complex powerful societies. By 300 BC, they were able to put armies of 50,000 and more mounted warriors into battle, and scored so many significant victories against the Chinese that the latter built a series of Great Walls to keep them out. Their weaponry and battle tactics were among the most sophisticated and successful in the world.

At the heart of their culture was the horse. Horse-riding gave them the freedom to roam over vast tracts of land. It gave them the power to make lightning strikes against their enemies and to outrun their pursuers in retreat. With this new-found freedom they abandoned fixed settlements and lived in circular tents, carrying their children and baggage in carts. Their womenfolk became superb riders, too, some of them taking up arms and becoming warriors, the original 'Amazons'.

The peoples of central Asia — the 'barbarians' — were at first renowned as archers, able to fire their arrows accurately from their galloping horses. By Roman times they had become armoured cavalry, using lances, scale armour and long, slashing swords. They were known to be fearless warriors who considered themselves equal or superior to anyone on earth. Their traditions owed nothing to the classical worlds of Europe — they had their own gods and spirits, priests and prophets. The most powerful of their gods was the god of war, who took the form of a magic sword. Their greatest glory was to die in battle, although those who did not do so sometimes opted to change their sex, to dress as women and become transsexual seers.

In the first millennium BC, the sight of a tight wedge of these fearsome mounted warriors charging into battle had struck fear into the hearts of almost all the 'civilized' peoples who had opposed them, from Assyria, Palestine and the very frontiers of ancient Egypt, right across the heart of Asia to the emerging Chinese Empire in the Far East.

The Romans were quick to realize that these particular 'barbarians' were formidable opponents, and that a more subtle approach would serve their empire best when it came to dealing with the warriors from the East. From the earliest days, the Romans sought ways of accommodating, exploiting and even recruiting them into their services. Several methods emerged, ranging from the straightforward contracting of mercenary cavalry units from the nomads to the forced relocation of war-prisoners and demands for the supply of warriors as tribute payment by defeated nomad leaders. This led to the dispersal of these mounted Eastern barbarians throughout the Roman Empire, as far afield as Spain, North Africa, northern France (inhabited then by Bretons and known as Armorica), and even to the northern frontiers of the Roman province of *Britannum*.

So the Eastern barbarians were deployed to control the antics of the other subject barbarians of the Roman Empire, even at its westernmost extremity in Britain. They did not come naked, nor on foot; they came heavily armed, on horseback. And they must have brought with them the customs, beliefs, stories and dreams which could forge a new world order, a way of shaping the world after the dust had settled on the bones of the fallen Roman Empire. Could it be that these 'barbaric' dreams eventually found their purest expression in the tales of the great king Arthur?

We all feel we have a clear, instinctive grasp of the contrast between civilized and barbaric behaviour. We have no problems distinguishing the savagery of Attila the Hun, Genghis Khan, the Nazis or even Serb paramilitaries from the civility of classical Greece and Rome, the Renaissance and the advanced democracies of the latter half of the twentieth century. It is axiomatic that *we* are civilized and *they* are barbarians. This is more than just an intellectual construct, it is a point of faith, a belief.

In fact, there is little objective historical truth in this idea. For

2000 years the line has been shot that our peace and security has been repeatedly threatened by some ghastly, savage 'other', all too often emanating from the East. One of the deepest appeals of king Arthur is that he is a defender of our Western faith, the quintessential hero figure, doing battle unto death against the forces of evil and chaos. The 'barbarians' in his tales are Saxons, dark forces threatening to overwhelm him and his kingdom, invading from the east. But in fact Arthur would have been viewed through Roman eyes as a pure bred barbarian himself.

Meanwhile the villains of his tales – the Saxons – can lay far better claim to being our true ancestors than any Celto-British warlord or king. After all, we still speak their language, use their names, live in their hamlets and towns. Exactly who is civilized and who a barbarian depends very much on whose historical perspective you are looking from. There is ample evidence throughout history for barbarians behaving in thoroughly civilized ways, and at least as much evidence for civilized peoples behaving with appalling barbarity. In my view, the maintenance of these artificial distinctions has acted as a barrier in coming to grips with the real forces which shaped the medieval world and, very probably, the legends of king Arthur.

So, if we are going to get at the truth we will need to penetrate beyond the myopic Roman mask of the 'civilized' versus the 'barbarian' and assess the players on the Dark Age stage on their own merits. The natural starting point in the search for Arthur lies within the 'barbarian' world he is said to have inhabited, the world of Celtic-speaking Britain.

CHAPTER TWO

Arthur's World

Celtic Britain

THE BRITONS, SOMETIMES ALSO CALLED THE INSULAR CELTS, WERE IN control of most of Britain from about 700 BC until the coming of the Romans, then resumed control after the Romans withdrew around AD 410. During the period when Arthur is said to have ruled – the late fifth to early sixth century AD – they held power but succumbed steadily to the encroachment of Germanic tribes invading from mainland Europe – Angles, Saxons and Jutes.

As a child, I always assumed that Arthur spoke English – he was after all the founder of the British nation, our backbone. And anyway I had seen him talking English on our brand new black-and-white telly and heard him on the radio, so the thought never crossed my mind that if he had lived when people said he did, then he would have spoken Gaelic, or Celtic. English was in fact the language of Arthur's deadliest enemies, the Saxons. Their eventual success in driving the British to the westernmost margins of the islands ensured the dominance of their language and gave it the tenacity to absorb first Nordic speakers (Danes and Vikings) then French speakers (Normans) before emerging as the language of Chaucer and Caxton, the first printer of Arthur's tales. But 2000 years ago, the language spoken by the British was assuredly a form of Celtic, closely related to the tongues of nearby Gaul (modern France), Iberia (Spain) and Eire (Ireland).

There is almost nothing in Britain which is as it was 2000 years ago, be it natural or man-made. Our impact on the landscape has been so great that only a few rocky crags and peaks, some rugged stretches of coastline, and perhaps a little unmolested woodland remain as they were at the time of Christ. But the process of altering the landscape had begun many millennia before Christ's times. The first farmers began to clear the land around 4000 BC and by the year zero about half of Britain's woodlands had been cleared for pasture or farmland. Temperatures at the turn of the millennium were two to three degrees centigrade warmer than they are now, allowing trees to grow rather higher on the hills and making the summers a little longer and warmer, winters a little milder than today.

The land was not only marked by clearance and settlement, but many of Britain's early peoples were great monument-builders. Stone circles, henges and barrows were scattered all over the land, signalling religious aspirations, astronomical expertise and reverence for the dead. Great ditch and mound earthworks – places of shelter and defence in times of war – capped many of the cleared hills. Tracks and trails wound their way between communities, marking lines of communication and exchange. There were even unfathomably mysterious landmarks such as Stonehenge, Avebury, and the enormous circular step pyramid of Silbury Hill, built in 2600 BC, at the same time that the ancient Egyptians were just beginning to build step pyramids on a far smaller scale. These man-made landmarks – striking, ancient and mysterious – were sure to find their way into the myths and legends of the Celtic peoples who colonized Britain from about 700 BC. They certainly found their way into the Arthurian written legends 2000 or so years later.

If the Celtic British were indeed Arthur's people, living in his era, then we must return to this world to seek out the roots of his stories. This is not so easily done. Before the coming of the Romans, the Celtic British were not literate. The Romans both recorded their own observation of the Britons, and taught them to write. But precious little has survived from Roman Britain, written in Latin by British hands, and what has survived usually has a Roman bias in its content. After all, only very Romanized Britons would have learnt to read and write in Latin. The archaeological record is extensive and helpful for this period, but the ideas communicated by objects alone are all too often ambiguous without historical, recorded information to guide our interpretations.

We are entirely reliant on Roman descriptions of what Gallic and British life was like, so once again the problem of bias is to the fore. Julius Caesar wrote extensively and insightfully about his adversaries in the Gallic wars, but he is best remembered for his pronouncement of the conquest of Britain *'Veni, vidi, vici'* – 'I came, I saw, I conquered' – but neither he nor any other Roman managed to conquer Britain for a further century after 55 BC.

Around AD 96, the Roman historian Tacitus published an account of his father-in-law's term of office in Britain. The *Agricola* gives many insights into the Roman Consul's subjects, the Britons. At the same time, Tacitus also published his *Germania*, a description of the German tribes living north of the Roman frontier, the Rhine-Danube barrier. This work contains information about the Celtic peoples of the European mainland, as do the later writings of Ammianus Marcellinus. Beside these descriptive works, numerous classical figures, from Cicero to Livy, took delight in proclaiming their superiority to the Gallic barbarians, and almost every emperor and administration left records relating to their governance of the Gallic lands and peoples, including Britain. Overall, then, we can build up a fair picture of Celtic life and thought at the dawn of the new millennium, although it is always essential to be aware that these Roman views are both 'spun' and 'seen from the outside'.

The Celts came to prominence in Europe before the rise of the Roman Empire. Apparently originating in southern Austria, they had then spread out in almost all directions. They made colonies as far east as the Black Sea and for a while occupied much of northern Italy. They moved westwards in large numbers, too, occupying France, much of the Iberian peninsula and almost all of the British Isles. By 390 BC, they were so militarily powerful that they actually burnt and pillaged much of the city of Rome, although they never really subjugated the Romans. In the long run, this was to prove their downfall as it was their Italian neighbours who eventually brought them to heel.

They were village farmers, growing cereals, a few vegetables and rearing livestock – sheep, goats, pigs, cattle and horses. Like everyone in the world in those days they knew how to hunt and fish, although these activities were not always important for subsistence. They were accomplished artisans, embracing the iron age and elaborating a decorative artistic style which flourished for 1000 years and is still familiar to us today. Their animals provided them with meat, leather, bone, milk, wool and the means to draw the plough, cart and chariot. They were good riders, a skill they probably acquired from the peoples of eastern Europe and the steppes. Their ponies were small but hardy. Among their livestock, cattle were the most valuable and desired of animals – a measure of wealth and a primary target for raiding.

They also knew how to build boats and rafts, and to navigate rivers and coastal waters. They crossed regularly from Britain to both continental Europe and Ireland. Much the same conditions pertained both before and after the Roman conquest, in Arthur's times, although little attention is paid to the basics of subsistence in the written Arthurian canon.

They lived mostly in villages, clusters of huts with stone or wattle walls and thatched roofs. A defensive outer wall, ditch or fence usually enclosed their settlements. Although they certainly had holy places they did not build enduring churches or temples, nor fortifications made of stone. The basic item of dress was a long cloak, held together at the neck with a brooch or pin. Wealthy male leaders also wore close-fitting linen shirts and trousers. Women wore loose-fitting skirts and blouses under their cloaks. We know little of their culinary arts, although they clearly made bread and gruel from their grain, roasted and boiled their meat, and were partial to mead, fermented watery honey.

In much of lowland Britain the climate was mild enough for agriculture to be a pretty reliable supplier of the year's needs, with surpluses stored at harvest time and animals killed off towards the end of the Celtic year – 31 October, our Hallowe'en. But in the upland and more northerly parts of the British Isles the climate was colder, the growing season shorter, and agriculture was only just feasible. An over-wet spring or autumn could ruin a crop, leaving the people in danger of starvation. It was probably because of the inhospitality of the land that the Romans never bothered to complete their conquests of Scotland and Wales, just as the Britons did not attempt to dislodge their hostile northern neighbours, the Picts and Caledonii. Their lands were of little value but their economic insecurity seemed to have a predictable effect on their outlooks. Perhaps out of necessity the Picts and Caledonii were very bold and warlike, forced to raid south in times of food shortage. They were also opportunistic, constantly striking at times of political and military upheaval in what is now England. Either way, they were a pain in the sides of both Britons and Romans.

The Celtic British world was not confined to these islands alone though. I have already mentioned that the Britons were quite capable of sailing to mainland Europe and to Ireland, and they certainly maintained trade relations with their continental Celtic cousins. This hooked them into networks which stretched all over Europe, from Scandinavia, across the Hungarian plain towards central Asia and from the Black Sea through the Balkans to the southern Alps, right across France and westwards into Iberia, where the very name Portugal (port of the Gauls) betrays a long-standing Celtic presence.

At the ends of these trade networks, the Celtic-speaking peoples of Europe were in direct touch with Rome and Greece, and through them with ancient Egypt, the Near East and North Africa. To the east, the furthest Celtic colonies mingled with the nomads of central Asia, and to the north there was constant contact – friendly or otherwise – with the Germanic-speaking peoples of what is now Germany, Poland, Hungary and Scandinavia. These were networks where not just goods but people and ideas flowed constantly. To give just two examples of the fluidity of the thought-lines of those times: excavations of pre-Roman London have yielded up a statue of the Egyptian goddess Isis from the mud of the river Thames, and the Gundestrup Cauldron – arguably the most important Celtic work of art from this entire era – was unearthed in a peat bog in Denmark, but it was apparently manufactured by Celts or Dacians living near to the Black Sea around 200 BC.

From the earliest times there seems to have been especially close bonds between the people we now call Bretons, inhabitants of modern-day Brittany, and the insular British. This closeness persisted for thousands of years and was certainly a very important factor in the assembly and dissemination of the various versions of the Arthurian legends in the Middle Ages. In Roman times, Brittany was known as Armorica.

The zenith of Celtic culture was in the fourth century BC and it was focused in France. There, village life expanded with the creation of substantial towns as craft specialization developed. The Celts were excellent metal-workers, in bronze, iron, silver and gold. Their smiths were certainly an élite who took great pride in their work, introducing the maker's stamp, or hallmark, to their finest pieces, especially their swords.

They had also developed great skill as wood-workers – building houses, fencing, ploughs, carts and even fine lightweight chariots out of wood. They modified the native woodlands of north-west Europe to meet their requirements for timber. On the one hand they protected great hardwoods like the oak, for use in boat- and house-building. On the other, they developed the system of coppic-ing, which provided them with poles for use as weapon hafts, fences, basketry and wattle-and-daub house walls.

They also had the time and skill to embellish their weapons, tools and jewellery with the characteristic swirling semi-abstract designs, which are familiar to us today. The archaeological record confirms that, although local traditions mushroomed in different parts of Celtic Europe at different times, all these skills were broadly shared throughout the Celtic world, including Britain.

Complementing this level of technical complexity, Celtic society was divided into three ranks – first, nobles, including paramount chiefs, war leaders and kings; second, common freemen, and third, slaves. Caesar labelled the nobles or aristocrats *equites*, horsemen, a label which has obvious resonances when considering the origins of both chivalry and the Arthurian legends. The fact that skill and pride in horsemanship was a Celtic virtue cannot be denied, although these skills seemed to have been concentrated among the Iberian Celts.

Freemen were typically farmers or artisans who served militarily as infantry. Slaves were often originally war captives, although they were also frequently bought and sold. They performed menial tasks, but we should note that they did not play the pivotal role in sustaining the economy that they performed within the Roman Empire. They also had an important part to play in some of the Celts' more extreme ritual practices. Privileged status was granted to a range of specialists – magicians or Druids, bards, poets, metal-workers, musicians, lawyers and doctors.

Most scholars doubt that the people we call Celts ever had a notion of being 'Celtic'. This was a term applied by outsiders to denote a huge array of people who shared a broadly similar language, culture and ideological system. We might compare it today with the way that colonial Europeans spoke of Africans or Indians. All well and convenient for them, but not a term that individuals from those continents would use to describe their identity.

The unit of self-identity in Celtic Europe was much smaller than 'pan-Celtic'. Caesar used the term *civitas* to denote this. It is usually translated as 'tribe', but I have great reservations about using a term which is now so value-laden with implications of primitiveness. Rather, given the 'civic' root of Caesar's term, 'nation' or perhaps 'community' or 'people' might be more appropriate. To give one example of a *civitas*, when Caesar conquered the Helvetii, ancestors of the Swiss nation (their current self-name is 'Communes Helvetiques'), they numbered about 265,000 people and were ruled over by their own king.

The way the political system worked was that each *civitas* was divided into smaller units, each presided over by a lord or noble, an *equitus*. Powerful and successful nobles exercised overlordship over less fortunate individuals, just as powerful kings could demand submission and allegiance from lesser royals. The whole system was bound together by notions of patronage and clientage. A (noble) patron provided his client with protection and support as well as land, livestock, tools and so on. In return, the client 'paid' his patron with food-rent, loyalty and military service. The more the clients, the more powerful the patron, be he the local village chief or the high-king of several *civitates*.

In theory this should have been a stable model of social organization. In practice it was not. Since the Celts did not adhere to strict inheritance rules like primogeniture, every time a notable died his fiefdom was up for grabs. Raiding, feuding and even warfare were commonplace as aspirants jockeyed for power with their rivals. This left the political system essentially fluid and open to manipulation, both from within or by determined outsiders, who could form alliances with one faction, in order to overcome another, then turn upon their new-found allies. Caesar repeatedly stresses that the Gauls are 'easily induced to form new plans and generally welcome political change'.

This, I should say from the start, is precisely the sort of political history we know to have been played out all over Celtic Europe, especially in Britain, both before the coming of the Romans, during their stay, and especially after their departure, in the days of Arthur. It is also precisely the political scenario in which the earlier parts of

Arthur's story were cast when they were committed to paper in the twelfth to fifteenth centuries. All the Arthurian legends chart his rise to power by a combination of battling and alliance-building with the rival kings of the various British regions.

This sense of intense insecurity, of the constant struggle to gain and maintain the ascendant in the quicksands of shifting political and military alliances, provides much of the dramatic impetus of the Arthurian legends. But it is also important to note that this sort of political organization, generating its own historical outcomes, is very widespread indeed. It is, after all, the way the English created their empire, cunningly exploiting the principles of 'divide and rule' across India, Africa and Asia. And it was – and is – the bread and butter of politics in almost every nation that is not centrally controlled. Take a close look, for example, at how people such as the Tuareg in the Sahara or their Berber ancestors, or the Swat Pathans in Afghanistan and their Indo-Iranian ancestors, ran and still run their political affairs, and you will see precisely the same model in action today as 2000 years ago. And, in my view, when we put the playing of political games in the Arthurian legends under the microscope, we can detect more precise elements in their behaviour which may not derive directly from the Celtic *civitas* model of political action.

Although in general women were politically subordinate to men, their role was not so rigidly defined as to totally exclude them from taking the initiative. For example, after her daughters were raped and she was flogged by the Romans, queen Boadicea (Boudica) of the British Iceni rose up in rebellion and rallied thousands of male soldiers to her standard. The Brigantes, a powerful and rebellious people living in what is now Yorkshire and Northumberland, also had a queen called Cartimandua. The woman's role in British society, then, was a good deal more flexible than in Roman society, where women were rarely better than second-class citizens.

However, having pointed that out, it would be impossible to argue that the elevated position accorded to women through the chivalric code and in the notion of courtly love, so prevalent in the Arthurian legends, has its roots in Celtic culture. What can be said is that Celtic British culture was flexible enough to allow those who aspired – whether male or female – to greatness to get their chance. Social status was not immutably fixed at birth and the potential to rise or fall in rank was open to all.

One way in which young men could enhance their status was through the war band. Men were not allowed to marry until they had inherited land, which meant that there were always young, unattached men in circulation. A young man could greatly enhance his prestige by leading his age-mates on a successful raid for cattle, prisoners, or treasure. These were the main sources and measures of wealth – the three basic units of 'currency' were a female slave, a cow and an ounce of silver.

Amassing wealth in the form of slaves, cattle and treasure was the goal of the Celtic political system, manifested in the display of fine jewellery, ornaments and weaponry. The context of the display was feasting and the entertaining of guests, served by slave women and entertained by bards, poets, story-tellers and musicians. Feasting and entertaining were essential for the formation and maintenance of alliances, which were often secured by marriage, but also the stage on which etiquette could be breached, anger flair and hostility spill over into vicious fighting. The Arthurian legends bristle with such incidents.

As fighting and warfare play such a huge part in the legends, we need to take a close look at what we know about martial behaviour as it really occurred in ancient Britain. Most of the Roman writers play on the Gallic love of war, and all stress how frightening it was to face their armies. Although some warriors wore chain-mail shirts – mail may have been a Celtic invention – many went into battle entirely naked except for their jewellery and weapons. Their sheer physical prowess was said to intimidate their enemies.

Challenges to single combat and actual individual fights were often precursors to mass action. Battles were invariably accompanied by a great deal of yelling, the blowing of loud trumpets and the banging of arms on shields. Caesar uses the term 'ululation' to describe their war-cries. The initial action was usually to hurl volleys of heavy spears at the enemy. These would either impale the opponent or get deeply embedded in his shield, thus greatly reducing his freedom of movement and ability to protect himself. Celtic shields were large and generally made of wood, covered with leather, and sometimes elaborated with metal. They covered more than half of the body, but Caesar did not consider them adequate protection.

In the last centuries BC, nobles went to war in two-horse chariots, accompanied by a chariot-driver and a steward who would help his lord to shelter if he were wounded in battle. The initial charge was aimed at breaking the enemy's line. After that, the chariot would come to a halt and the noble would dismount to do battle on foot. Around 200 BC, chariots were largely replaced by mounted cavalry on mainland Europe as Celtic riding and mounted martial skills developed. Caesar was pleased to discover that the British continued to rely heavily on outmoded chariots in their efforts to repulse him in 55 and 54 BC.

A general mêlée followed the initial charge, the main aim being to force a rout. If this did not succeed, then the combatants slogged it out until one side got the upper hand. As battles mostly took place in open ground the outcome was rarely an 'orderly retreat'. Rather the losers broke ranks and tried to head for cover in woods, high ground or marshy land. The victors gave hot pursuit and cut down or captured as many of the enemy as they could.

This pattern of warfare was all well and good when Celt fought fellow Celt or German but when they came up against the superior discipline of the Roman legions and the tactical skill of the Roman commanders, their shock tactics did not always work. Roman arms were specifically designed for maximum efficacy in close-quarter fighting. The Romans carried large shields which could be held together to create an almost impenetrable wall against volleys of spears or arrows. Their long spears could be used to good effect against charging cavalry or charioteers, and their heads, faces and torsoes were well protected by armour. Their short swords were specifically designed for stabbing the enemy in a close maul and could be wielded in very confined spaces.

By contrast, many Celts and Britons did not wear armour at all; their swords were long slashing weapons with blunt points, well suited to single-combat duels or fighting in an open ruck, but they were useless for stabbing, and their length made them difficult to wield in confined space.

In terms of the infantry, the Romans soon discovered that they had the upper hand when they combined their fighting skills with cunning tactics. For their part, the Celts seemed almost insulted by the discipline and guile of their enemies. A delegation from the Celtic Helvetii actually rebuked Caesar for attacking their kinsmen at night as they tried to cross a river:

> He had made a surprise attack on one clan at a moment when
> their comrades who had crossed the river could not come to
> their help; but he should not on that account exaggerate his
> own prowess or despise them. They had learned from their
> fathers and ancestors to fight like brave men, and not to rely on
> trickery or stratagem.

Several Roman commentators remarked on the psychological effects
of chariot warfare. Being charged by two powerful war horses, the
chariot wheels producing a fearsome din, was unnerving for the
foot-soldier. But chariots are at best unstable machines, tipping over
very easily on rough ground. There are countless reports in antiquity,
from Assyria to China, of kings and nobles being pitched out of their
chariots and of horses careering out of control. It was virtually
impossible to fire arrows or hurl spears from them while on the
move, and their only real contribution was to provide mobility while
in the field. Most of us have seen *Ben Hur* and witnessed the thrill of
chariots in action, and this perhaps provides the key to the essentially
ritual role of this vehicle. Chariots were ideal for display, for parading
in triumph down the Appian Way, for the great public show of
martial valour, but they were of very limited use as vehicles of war.

Cavalry, however, could be the deciding factor in warfare in those
days and the Celts were certainly good horsemen. The Greek
geographer Strabo wrote:

> The whole race of Gauls is madly fond of war. Although they
> are fighters by nature they are better as cavalry than as infantry.

When the Gauls set out to assault Rome in 390 BC, they were said to number 5000 infantry and 20,000 cavalry (ratio 5:2). This should be compared to the Roman legion, typically comprising about 5000 troops, of whom only 200 were cavalry in the early centuries of the Empire (ratio 50:2). But important though the cavalry were, the Gauls and Britons, lacking stirrups (which are essential if you intend to use a lance in mounted offence and not fall off), mainly deployed them as skirmishers and on the infantry's flanks.

In many cases, while the battle was being slugged out, cavalrymen would dismount and go into battle on foot. Spanish Gauls even attached a special peg to their horses' reins which they drove into the ground, thus tethering their mounts while joining the fray. But if the tide went their way, they remounted and were at their deadliest in hot pursuit of retreating enemies, where the ability to run down the fleeing infantry greatly increased the death rate in battle.

It is clear that in the centuries leading up to the Roman conquest of Gaul and Britain cavalry were not deployed in headlong frontal assaults. The heavy cavalry charge – the core of the Arthurian mode of battle – had not yet been invented. This situation would change, however, during the course of the Roman occupation of Britain.

Besides open warfare on the battlefield, the Britons – following a tradition which even pre-dates the arrival of Celtic peoples in Britain – also built and manned strong hill forts for defensive purposes. Although most forts dating from this period have been worn away by centuries of ploughing, some do still survive – great ringed ramparts and ditches encircling the tops of open hills. Some of these earthworks were so large that they contained both living quarters and grazing for cattle and horses. They were evidently used as assembly points during wars, where a large part of the local population could congregate under the protection of their menfolk. Hills selected for these sites were usually extremely steep on all but one side, so that they could be lightly defended on the steep sides with a concentration of defences on the one approachable slope.

Gauls and Britons did not just dig ditches and pile up the dirt to make ramparts, as they appear today, they made well-constructed stone and wood barrier walls and sometimes capped them with wooden walls and palisades. Within the stockades, the populous would have been well protected, although in many cases withstanding sieges must have been severely limited by a lack of water. Many of the most famous surviving hill forts were built in southern and south-west Britain on the tops of downland chalk hills where there was no chance of digging wells for water. In fact, the idea of taking up defensive positions to withstand a siege seems to me to go against the grain of the British approach to warfare. Consequently their knowledge of siege warfare appears to have been limited.

Caesar describes sending in his infantry, their large shields forming a protective 'roof' over their heads, to build up earth mounds against the British fort walls then overrunning them. In other battles it is clear that the British lacked the Romans' ingenuity at laying siege with battering rams, ballistas and the like. On his second campaign Caesar – who wrote his memoirs in the third person – came upon the hill fort of the British war overlord Cassivellaunus:

> . . . protected by forests and marshes, filled with a large number of men and cattle. (The Britons apply the term 'stronghold' to densely wooded spots fortified with a rampart and trench, to which they retire to escape the attacks of invaders.) He marched to the place with his legions, and found that it was of great natural strength and excellently fortified. Nevertheless, he proceeded to assault it on two sides. After a short time the enemy proved unable to resist the violent attack of the legions and rushed out of the fortress on another side. A quantity of

cattle were found there and many of the fugitives were captured and killed.

Although I have no doubt that Caesar has greatly over-simplified the ease with which he took the fort, there are so many accounts of Roman victories after sieges that this inability to create and hold good defensive positions seems to be a major reason for the rapid collapse of Gallic resistance once the Roman onslaught had begun.

There is archaeological evidence for the resumption of using hill forts in post-Roman Britain in the fifth century AD, as the Britons fought among themselves and took on the invading Saxons. But by the time people began to write down the Arthurian legends 600 years later, the hill fort had been entirely superseded by the stone castles of the Normans and their successors.

These stone castles, with their vertical dressed walls, portcullises, surrounding moats, drawbridges and the like, are the enduring stage-set for the Arthurian dramas and the very medieval patterns of conflict which unfold within and without the castle walls. Sieges recur frequently but they are usually stoutly defended and resistance is prolonged, reflecting the historical truth that well-defended castles were very difficult to take by force in the late Middle Ages. In this respect, Arthur's chroniclers made little effort to 'set the stage' in Dark Age Britain, with its hill forts, preferring instead to dream up a Gothic Camelot which Tennyson and Walt Disney would later adopt – all sheer stone walls, conical turrets, battlements and drawbridges. Romantically delightful and visually inspiring as these are, they are artifices of late medieval Britain and have nothing to do with the Dark Ages – Arthur's times.

Working my way through the Roman literature on politics, diplomacy and warfare with the Gauls and Britons, I noticed one very standard procedure which all parties seemed to have adhered to: the giving of hostages. As a means of ensuring the continuity of alliances with partners you do not entirely trust, it was a smart and frequently employed move to demand that your ally's wife, children, even entire family be placed in your care. The Romans made this demand endlessly of the 'barbarian' chiefs and kings they did not trust, but it was also a widely used tactic between Gallic and British leaders.

Curiously, the giving of hostages is not an important motif in Arthurian legends, as the practice seems to have died out once most of Britain was unified under a single king. Although alliances are cemented by marriage (Guinevere was the queen of the Summer Country, Somerset) it seems that allegiance had become more a matter of honour, of obedience to an ethical code (chivalry) which demanded loyalty to a leader, rather than using hostages as a form of insurance of that loyalty. In return, the leader was expected to be generous to his subjects – rewarding them with land and treasure.

Once again, the *realpolitik* of the late medieval world was transposed into the Arthurian legends with little regard for historical veracity, although I think the motives for excluding hostage-taking were probably not to do with a lack of knowledge of these practices. Copies of Caesar's *De Belli Gallici* were certainly available to the writers of the legends, many of whom took pride in their scholarship, but their exclusion of hostage-taking may have been on ethical grounds. The problem arises when things go wrong. If a trusted ally turns coats, then it is the hostage-holder's prerogative to butcher the hostage-giver's family. This certainly happened repeatedly in the Dark Ages, but cutting the throats of innocent babes and gentlewomen hardly fits the heroic gloss with which the writers sought to embellish Arthur.

There is another practice associated with war which I suspect Arthur's chroniclers would have chosen to leave out of the ancestral repertoire: human sacrifice. We have grisly evidence for this practice from the bog people, executed victims whose bodies were immersed in peat. Although they are most common among the Germanic peoples of Scandinavia, Germany and the Low Countries, they have also been found in northern England and Ireland. The most famous British specimen, 'Pete Marsh' or Lindow Man, had been struck twice on the skull, once in the back, and then garrotted before having his throat cut in what may have been an act of blood-letting. This 'triple killing' had distinctive Celtic roots, where it is known that people were sacrificed both to divine the outcome of warfare, and as offerings to the goddess of fertility.

By the sixth century AD, Christianity had made its way to Britain, although it was far from universally accepted and the Saxon invaders were still pagans. This thin veneer of Christianity, overlaying traditional Celtic religious mores, was, I think, quite accurately reflected in the written Arthurian canon. All the authors are at pains to give Arthur the trappings of Christianity, making him a king who attends mass several times a day, and surrounded by bishops, monasteries, monks and the like, but there is little Christian in the fabric of the tales. The closest the chroniclers come to this is in the enormously long and elaborate quests for the Holy Grail.

Tales associating holy chalices and (the drinking of) human blood are known to have existed in many parts of Europe from the earliest times. In fact, it seems that, like many Arthurian motifs, the Grail Quest is a Christian gloss on a very widespread sacred chalice cult. As mentioned earlier in this chapter, perhaps the most famous chalice in antiquity is the Gundestrup Cauldron, probably made by Celtic craftsmen in the Black Sea area around 200 BC. This magnificent object was carefully dismantled by its Germanic owners (probably members of the Cimbri people) and placed as a votive offering in a peat bog in Denmark. One of its panels portrays a line of warriors; and, following the outline of the tree of life at its top, they pass a dog (symbol of death) and are lifted up by an enormous god who lowers them gently into a large cauldron. Above and in front of the cauldron, a line of mounted warriors ride away from the life-transforming scene, as if reborn as cavalrymen.

We know from other sources that the Celts believed in rebirth – Caesar considered their recklessness in battle to be a direct result of their contempt for death and belief in rebirth – and this extraordinary scene on the cauldron appears to portray the means of achieving this rejuvenation, perhaps even improvement, as foot-soldiers are magically transformed into horsemen.

In fact, we will come across so many examples of 'pagan' motifs in the written legends that it is clearly important to establish where these motifs have sprung from – whether they are in fact Celtic in origin. To do this we need to sketch out the salient features of Celtic British religious ideology.

As the pre-Roman Celtic world was not literate we have very little written information on this subject, especially as far as the peculiarities of British beliefs are concerned. Roman observers concentrated more on ritual practices (events they could observe) than on mythology or cosmology, although they do provide some important insights into Celtic ideas surrounding death and the afterlife.

The archaeological record provides images of the Celtic pantheon and some evidence of ritual events, and there are two other important sources which scholars use to flesh out the Celtic supernatural world – the ancient myth cycles of the Welsh and Irish. These epic tales provide brilliant insights into the ways in which ancient Celts conceived the Otherworld, and the sorts of characters and events which peopled it – but for our purposes they must be treated with caution.

Although the tales contain elements which suggest they had existed in oral form for centuries before, they were only actually written down at about the same time as the Arthurian legends were being transcribed in England and France. Some of the Irish material can be traced back to the sixth and seventh centuries AD, but none of it can be derived from the period when the classical writers were at work, nor to the period when Arthur was said to have lived. Although we do encounter our hero, Arthur, going out on an epic quest with his cousin in the Welsh *The Spoils of Annwn*, this tale first made it on to the page in the thirteenth century, a century after another Welshman, Geoffrey of Monmouth, first brought Arthur to the English literate world's attention.

Holding these reservations in mind, we can outline the Celtic spiritual perspective in some detail. Like all other people living at the same time as them, the Celts had a clear vision not just of the world of the living, but of an Otherworld, where time stood still. It was the home of ancestors, of the souls of the dead and of deities, and it was the place of regeneration. These two worlds were not entirely separate, however. People of advanced spiritual knowledge – Druids among the living, mythical heroes, spirits and even gods and goddesses – could cross between the two worlds, although it was perilous to do so.

In Irish mythology, the Otherworld could be reached by sailing to the west (out into the Atlantic). Elsewhere a common 'gateway' was downwards, either in caves, tunnels and shafts or under water. Springs, wells, lakes, waterfalls, marshes and peat bogs all provided access to the Otherworld, the centre of rebirth. In a slightly different way, trees also mediated between worlds, with their roots sunk firmly in the underworld, their trunks in the world of the living and their crowns touching the celestial sky, home to the most powerful god of all, the sun. Trees also possessed the magical qualities of death and regeneration. In autumn they 'die', shedding their leaves and taking on skeletal form; in spring they are reborn, clothed in leaves; and in late summer, at the height of the year, they even bear fruit – offspring. Arthur's destination on his journey beyond mortality was the magic Isle of Avalon, Island of the Apple Orchards.

Water and watery places, essential for the sustenance of all life forms, not only provided 'gateways' to the Otherworld, they were recognized as holy places – places of fecundity. Tacitus reports how in a great annual ritual the fertility goddess Nerthus was brought out of the water, placed in a cart and paraded round the countryside. While she was abroad, all military activity had to cease, all weapons concealed. Once her procession was complete, she returned to the waters, where all the slaves who had accompanied her were at once put to death by drowning. The Celts and Britons certainly had their 'Lady of the Lake', and she was not only associated with fertility, but with weaponry too.

In the lands of the Germanic and Celtic peoples throughout north-west Europe, the custom of depositing prized objects in water was extremely widespread. From Denmark to Switzerland, all over France and in Britain and Ireland, votive offerings were placed in lakes, rivers, marshes and peat bogs in the early centuries. These included human victims (bog people), ornaments and jewellery – such as torques and the famous Gundestrup Cauldron – and immense quantities of weapons. The weapons were nearly all deliberately damaged, in accordance with the belief that an object fit for the gods should be rendered unusable for the living.

Although Excalibur is not damaged in any of the Arthurian renderings, the yielding up of the magic sword to the water goddess is entirely in keeping with ancient British thinking and praxis. However, we should bear in mind that, although notions of throwing divine weapons to watery female deities is entirely consistent with ancient British cosmology, there are *no* examples of such an event in any of the recorded British (or Irish) myths prior to the Arthurian tales.

Cauldrons and chalices are in a sense miniature versions of ponds, lakes or springs. Liquid containers which could hold water, wine or human blood, they held the power to transform anyone who symbolically bathed in them by drinking their contents. Both the Irish and Welsh mythology have 'cauldrons of rebirth' which can restore dead warriors to life if they are cooked in it overnight. There is no doubt that the ancient British held the same views, but so did a large number of other peoples and cultures.

Although the early Celts and British were not great builders of sacred monuments (at least not ones which have survived to the present or caught the attention of the classical chroniclers), they were great believers in holy places. Typically they revered sacred groves, stands of trees set around watery places. Here would be the home of some nymph or perhaps goddess, where holy rites took place. Trees on these sites represented both sanctity, shelter or haven, and the physical manifestations of the cycles of life, death and rebirth.

These groves and glades are the archetypal setting for much of the action in Arthurian legends. Time and again, one or other of our heroes enters a glade, falls asleep by a stream, crosses a river or is accosted by a hostile knight who, as mentioned, is both guardian of the place and gaoler to a damsel. Battle ensues, the outcome sealing the fate of defendant, challenger and the damsel/nymph. I can see no alternative to attributing the setting for this common Arthurian scenario directly to the Celto-British notion of the holy glade or grove. However, when we come to assess what goes on in these holy places in Chapter Four, we will find that the action there is often not as it might have been in fifth-century Britain.

Presiding over these sacred places were the Druids. Caesar asserts that they were British in origin and that their cult spread from there to the continental Gauls. He says that their training could take twenty years and involved the learning of all manner of ancient tales, formulae and spells passed down from generation to generation. They were certainly influential people, and their role cut directly into the political world via their divinatory powers. Following traditions which may pre-date Celtic Britons, one important method of divination was human sacrifice by stabbing or strangulation, and the observation of both the death throes and the entrails of the victim.

Needless to say, these more macabre aspects of the Druids' role are not ascribed to Merlin in the Arthurian canon, although there are instances of a similar, gory ritual event: head-taking. This was sometimes in effect trophy-taking, a showing off of personal victory on the battlefield. But heads were important magical objects long before the Celts. The entrances to ancient hill forts were sometimes adorned with human heads on spikes to ward off evil and many single heads have been placed as votive offerings in wells and springs in Celtic times, even as late as the seventh century AD in Wales.

Severed heads are important symbols, then, in both Welsh and Irish mythology and there is some suggestion that they could have magical healing powers. In one Irish tale, a severed head takes on the properties of the Cauldron of Regeneration, when people who drink milk poured into the skull regain their strength. Similar events take place in the Arthurian legends with similar results, although again, as we shall see later, the severed head as a potent magical symbol is to be found well beyond the bounds of the Celtic world.

Returning to the Celto-British pantheon, there is some evidence that the sun-god was the supreme being, and many important Celtic dignitaries were buried with solar discs or wheels in their graves.

Perhaps more relevant for our purposes, the sun was thought to cross the firmament in a chariot pulled by divine horses. The Celts also had a horse goddess – Epona, her name derived from the Celtic word for horse, *epos*. Although not conceived of as a horse *per se*, she was the protectress of all cavalrymen, and seen as the goddess of horse fertility and breeding. She is always depicted with horses, either riding them or alongside them. Perhaps because of the Christian veneer gilding the written Arthurian sources, this divine horse-woman does not make an appearance.

Other animals were attributed with special supernatural powers. Stags, wild boar, ravens, bulls, as well as horses, all have special roles to play as manifestations, or close associates, of specific gods and goddesses. There is also some evidence for composite animals, where the 'qualities' of two or more species are brought together for magical purposes. Snakes with rams' horns are said to represent fertility and regeneration, and a particularly fine bull's head with an eagle head emerging between its horns symbolizes pure power. But in pre-Roman times the Celtic craftsmen did not take this 'composition' of mythical beasts to the great lengths that other cultures were creating at the time. Conspicuously absent from the mythical menagerie are dragons, griffins, centaurs, sphinxes and the like. This is an important absence, as various monsters and dragons appear repeatedly in the Arthurian written tales.

But for all the lack of specialized mythical beasts, Celtic British culture was robust and complex, an important member of the pan-European Celtic cultures which had stretched from the shores of the North Sea to Hungary and Asia Minor by the fourth century BC. Based upon powerful and enduring institutions, the principal means of the transmission of this culture from generation to generation was by oral tradition. Poets and bards made their tales known in rhyme, musicians in song and story-tellers abounded.

Celtic people revelled in story-telling, and stories have been the prime expression of their ethnic identity since very early times. In Ireland, where the tradition has been disrupted least, there are still people known as *Scianna chui*, 'story-tellers', living in the Gaeltacht on the western fringes of the island. In the 1980s, I was lucky enough to meet Dr Seamus O'Cathain of the Department of Irish Folklore at University College, Dublin, and he kindly introduced me to the staggering riches of the Irish oral tradition. There are several major myth cycles in Irish Gaelic, and his department holds up to 800 variants on each of the main stories. Almost every village in Ireland had its own version of every major story.

There was one memorable fable entitled 'The Man Who Had No Story'. It told of a traveller, weary and lost, who knocked on a cottager's door, begging for a little food and lodging for the night. The cottager welcomed him and offered him all he asked for as long as he could tell a story as payment. The traveller could not, so he suddenly found he had fallen through this world into the gloom of the Underworld. A succession of further calamities beset the man until eventually he has sufficient experiences to weave together a tale. So, in the end, it was the tale itself that saved him.

This delight in story-telling, in the transmission of experience from mind to mind via the tongue, is vitally important when we come to look for the true roots of the Arthurian legends. Many elements of these had obviously been handed down by word of mouth for generations before they were set down on vellum or parchment.

There is something unique about the Celtic mastery of words, just as their decorative art is immediately recognizable and distinctive. It is such a powerful element of the Celtic heart that it has survived all the jostling and bustling of two millennia, giving us in this century alone such master wordsmiths as Yeats, Joyce, Synge, Dylan Thomas and Seamus Heaney, to name but a few. It is also recognized repeatedly in the Arthurian tales where much of the content is taken up with Arthur ordering various knights to undertake quests and adventures. On their eventual return to court, Arthur invariably orders them to recount all that has happened to them, to tell their stories. He is acutely aware that it is through experience that we learn, and through the sharing of experience we grow wiser.

There is no doubt, then, that Arthur's stories are firmly rooted in the Celtic tradition of story-telling, but to what extent are the contents of the tales a reproduction of Celto-British culture from the Dark Ages or before? This is the question I set out to answer in this chapter and it is time to draw my findings together.

First, at its most simplistic, it is very clear that the tales as written down represent a fusion between the historical realities of the Dark Ages and those of the times when the actual documents were written down. We will look at this more closely in Chapter Three, where we will find that the stories change and develop between 1136 when Geoffrey of Monmouth wrote *The History of the Kings of England* and 1485, when Caxton published Malory's *Le Morte D'Arthur.*

These changes and developments accurately reflect changes in the cultures of the writers over a period of 350 years of European history. But, for now, the point is simply that many aspects of the written tales are drawn directly from the experience of the writers' daily lives and not from their knowledge of early (or even late) Celtic culture and history. In particular the physical settings – the court, the daily (Christian) religious observations, the spectacles of tourneys, and the pursuit of chivalry and courtly love – reflect directly the world of the twelfth to fifteenth centuries and not the world of the sixth century AD. The military aspects of the tales share the same skew – the absolute dominance of cavalry and indifference to infantry fits the historical record far better in the late Middle Ages than in Dark Age Britain.

In costume and dress, once again the written sources detail men and women in medieval clothes – and the men are bearded, whereas Caesar specifies that Gallic men shaved all of their bodies except for their heads and upper lips. Artistic depictions of Celtic men show them either with moustaches or beards. The weapons, armour, harnessing and adornment of the horses, described in the written sources, are also drawn from medieval times, although there is some continuity from the days of the Celts to the times of the writers. The Celts had long swords, mail armour and elaborate helmets, but they could not use heavy lances as they had no stirrups. Tilting and jousting would have been impossible for them until the stirrup arrived in Britain.

Although the Romans used martial decoration, I have not come across any evidence of the Celtic peoples using battle standards, flags or other forms of martial decoration other than on their shields and helmets. However, the Arthurian tales make many references to the use of both ordinary animals, such as the boar and the eagle, and mythical beasts, notably the dragon, as battle standards and the like. The placing of these symbols on battlements and towers atop smooth stone-walled castles, rife throughout the written sources, is yet another reflection of medieval times, whereas the Britons, both before and after the Romans, relied principally on earthworks as fortifications.

The portrayal of relations between kings and kingdoms, and between kings and their vassals, war leaders and their subordinates, are perhaps the most historically accurate aspects of the written sources, although elements of the feudal vassalage system are also infused in most of the tales. Slavery plays little part, probably because by medieval times straightforward ownership of people had been largely replaced by contractual systems binding serfs and villeins to their overlords. Similarly, the use of hostages as pawns in the political system is barely referred to in the written sources, probably because this form of political game-playing had become less relevant to the more stable, centrally controlled monarchies of medieval Europe. But playing host at feasts and celebrations, where conspicuous wealth and political prestige could be displayed, was still an important part of the 'great game' in medieval times, as it was in the Dark Ages.

Intriguingly, in the realms of the mystical and magic, there is a surprisingly high degree of 'match' between the written Arthurian world and Celtic conceptions. The quest for the Grail has only a very shallow gloss of Christianity. It fits much more easily into a worldview where the promise of eternal life rests in the Cauldron of Regeneration. Likewise, the central role of holy water, holy glades and their association with pure, white-clad females (Guinevere means white woman) unquestionably hailed directly from the Celtic past. The importance of severed heads, of blood and the potential healing powers of the severed head, all have Celtic roots too, although we will see that these deeply mystical ideas have a far wider currency than just the ancient Celtic world.

It is fascinating that so many of these extremely deep, murky motifs made their way into the writings of people who had espoused the Christian faith for at least several centuries before they put pen to paper. For me, this is evidence of the unprovable – that this esoteric mystical paganism must have been carried down the centuries in oral tradition. I have described how powerful and important myth-telling was for the Britons and their Celtic cousins. We know from the magnificent Beowulf and the Norse Sagas that the Saxons and later the Vikings greatly revered their oral traditions, too, that keeping the torch of the 'Golden Age' of mythic heroism burning was seen as a sacred, if not Christian, duty. These magical tales purported links with a supernatural past, a continuity of heritage which Christianity – an alien and aggressively proselytizing dogma – could never totally suppress. The safest, perhaps the only way to keep this magical world alive in a society dominated by a hostile doctrine was to whisper the tales down the generations from mouth to ear, ear to mouth.

Pagan mythology, as we will see in Chapter Three, was in a sense forced underground until such time as it became politically expedient to bring it back out into the open in a new secular form – the form of the tales of Arthur. For the pagan Britons, embracing the doctrine of life, death and rebirth, it seems entirely apt that their greatest king should never really die, becoming transformed instead into the 'Once and Future King'.

So far, then, there is a fairly good match between Dark Age Britain and its medieval chroniclers, allowing for a strong tendency to portray the distant past in contemporaneous terms. But we also need to turn this formula around and look at what we have *not* been able to find in the written sources of Celtic Britain. This is where the trouble starts . . .

If you ask people what they know of king Arthur, they will certainly reply, 'The sword in the stone . . . knights of the round table . . . Excalibur . . . Camelot . . . ' – and, perhaps, the Lady of the Lake, Merlin, Guinevere and Lancelot.

So where are these central icons – where are the very symbols which make the Arthurian legend what it is to most of us? These vital elements are simply missing from the world of the Celtic Britons who certainly did not have a sword god – and the idea of magical swords only appears in late Celtic mythology, stories which apparently post-date Arthur's times. Nor is there anywhere a reference to the drawing of a sword from a stone, even though it is such a powerful metaphor for the act of iron-making. Nowhere, too, is there a trace of round tables in our British past, and, although there are rival claims all over the British Isles, no one has proved that any particular site is Camelot.

Furthermore, although the Celts were certainly competent horsemen, there is no evidence that they developed and honed their mounted martial skills in the way that Arthur and his knights are reported to have done. In fact, the weight of evidence is that, other than the occasional charge, the Celts rarely fought on horseback, and lacked the technical requirements to form heavy cavalry units which could fight from the saddle. Yet it is impossible for any of us to imagine an Arthur who has to dismount before doing battle. Nor is there any evidence that the ancient Britons were the progenitors of the ideology which accompanied the rise of mounted martial skills.

Chivalry – the horseman's code – with its adherence to rules of honour, fairness and courtesy, is not a part of the Celtic canon, nor is the elevation of the fairer sex to a position of adoration a Celtic concept; and it certainly was not a Roman idea. As mentioned, Romans cared little for honour and courtesy, and even less for their womenfolk. Neither did the Romans know or care about swords in stones or cavalry skills – they continued to try to buy the services of foreign cavalry rather than develop the skills themselves. So, given that neither the Romans nor the Britons can provide us with the keys to discovering the origins of the most widely acclaimed aspects of the Arthurian tales, we will have to look elsewhere.

One likely place is precisely among the mercenary cavalry cohorts the Romans introduced to western Europe. One such group, a force under the command of a Roman general with the unusual name of Lucius Artorius Castus, was despatched to Britain in the late second century AD. Their battle standards were fiery dragons and they wore scale armour and carried long swords. They also knew stories of a legendary king who wielded a magic sword. But before we look at these people in detail we need to examine the hard evidence for the existence of a king or war leader named Arthur, as laid down on paper or determined in the archaeological record.

CHAPTER THREE

A Real Arthur?

The Evidence

. . . .
. . . .

IN THE 1200 YEARS OR SO THAT SCHOLARS HAVE BEEN ADDRESSING THE question of the existence of a real historical figure called Arthur, a consensus has been reached which allocates a place to him in the overall chronology of Dark Age Britain. Following the pseudo-historical accounts of his life and deeds, scholars have identified him at the end of the fifth and the beginning of the sixth century AD. This identification is not, however, based on written evidence, rather it is adduced, using the following train of thought: 'We know he didn't exist then because so-and-so was ruling at that time: then (later) We know that another figure was ruling at a later date, *ergo* Arthur must have ruled in the interim'. Alternatively: 'We know the Saxon advances were checked around this date, and the Arthurian tales tell us he defeated the Saxons. Therefore he must have led Britain at the time the Saxons were checked.' I cannot stress too strongly that it is only circumstantial evidence like this which leads some scholars to conclude that Arthur 'must have' existed. There is no irrefutable evidence that he did.

Scholars who do not accept Arthur as a historical figure of course reject this version of history, and do so with good reason, as the evidence supporting the claims of the pro-Arthur camp is extremely thin. The existing evidence is in fact so weak that it should be questioned right from the start. The first apposite question to ask is: did Arthur exist at all?

I am far from the first person to question whether he was ever anything more than a 'mighty shadow'. This is what William Caxton had to say in 1485, in his preface to Sir Thomas Malory's *Le Morte D'Arthur* :

> The said noble gentleman [Geoffrey of Bouillon] instantly required me to imprint the history of the said noble king and conqueror, King Arthur, and of his knights, with the history of the Sangrail and of the death and ending of the said Arthur, affirming that I ought rather to imprint his acts and noble feats, . . . considering that he was a man born within this realm, and king and emperor of the same; and that there be in French divers and many noble volumes of his acts, and also of his knights.
>
> To whom I answered, that divers men hold opinion that there was no such Arthur, and that all such books as be made of him be but feigned and fable, because that some chronicles make of him no mention nor remember him nothing, ne of his knights.
>
> Whereto they answered, and one in special said, that in him that should say or think that there was never such a king called Arthur might well be arreted great folly and blindness; for he said that there were many evidences of the contrary . . .

As Caxton made clear, almost from the moment the first written accounts of Arthur appeared they were denounced as fraudulent works of fiction by some, while others saw them as the revelation of a long-concealed but real secret history. To find out if this purported history is real or illusory we need to go back to the time when it is claimed that Arthur lived, and seek out what evidence exists to support this claim.

The first attempt to give a comprehensive account of Arthur's life and reign is in Geoffrey of Monmouth's *The History of the Kings of Britain,* completed in AD 1136. Although he is very vague about dates, his tale is a narrative, starting with the colonization of Albion by the Trojan Brutus and his followers who founded the British nation. It traces their history during the Roman occupation and on through the chaotic period which followed, arriving eventually at the high point of his 'history', the tale of Arthur.

Following Geoffrey's chronology, this placed Arthur's reign somewhere between AD 480 and AD 520. Even though the veracity of his account has been severely questioned from the day of its publication, the idea that Arthur lived around those dates has stuck. I would just point out that this acceptance is not based on facts. It is not a fact that Arthur reigned at that time any more than it is that he had a magic sword or was raised by the Druid Merlin. Yet there are some reasons, based on the better-established general history of this period, why this line of argument has been consistently supported.

The Romans withdrew from Britain at the beginning of the fifth century AD. During their occupation they had controlled virtually all of what is now England, though not all of Wales or Scotland. While dominating the Britons, they had not entirely destroyed their traditional social structure. Nobles, chiefs, even regional British kings, were left in place and often co-opted into the Roman administration. Many British nobles became rich enough to build their own villas, especially in southern Britain. Local people were also encouraged to join the Roman army as auxiliary forces. They were not only paid well, they gained full Roman citizens' rights on completion of their service.

This was all well and good while the Roman Empire remained stable, but at the end of the fourth century things started to go badly wrong for the Romans on the European mainland. Whole legions, including their (British) auxiliary troops, were ordered to the mainland to confront the various waves of barbarian invasions pressing at the Empire from the east and north-east. When they eventually gave up Britain in AD 410, the Romans left a country which was militarily very weak and lacking a centralized system of political control.

At the same time, continental Europe was entering a period of huge turmoil – the time of the Great Migrations. Whole populations were on the move, testing their mettle against friends and neighbours as well as traditional enemies and rivals. Any groups which were not well organized and co-ordinated were vulnerable, and this certainly applied to the newly abandoned Britons.

With the sudden departure of centralized control, the Britons reverted to the political system they had employed before the conquest. Local kings proclaimed themselves overlords and vied with each other for the greatest power and political control. Networks of alliances sprang up only to disintegrate with the death of a key player or the defection of a faction to another camp. The Picts, living in unconquered Scotland and the traditional enemies of the Celtic British, spotted the turmoil to the south and began sustained raids and attacks, both by land and sea.

According to tradition, one of the British leaders, a man named Vortigern ('Overking', the British equivalent of the Roman *Dux Bellorum*) made the fatal mistake of inviting the fierce Saxon peoples to come to his aid as mercenaries against the Picts. Once they had set foot in Britain, the Saxons quickly realized the weakness of the British and began to force themselves upon the land as invading colonists.

Whether Vortigern's part in these events is fact or fiction, the archaeological record attests to the arrival and settlement of Saxons, Angles, Jutes and Frisians all over eastern England, from Kent to Northumbria, during the fifth century. From there, they advanced steadily westwards, although both the archaeological record and the scant written sources show that they had to fight for their spoils. They also reveal that the Saxon advance was effectively halted for thirty to sixty years around the end of the fifth century. Conventionally Arthur is credited with this check in the Saxon advance.

The setback was only temporary, however. By the end of the sixth century Anglo-Saxons had overrun all of what is now England. During the course of that century many of the invaders had converted to Christianity and a few had become literate. With the British beaten back into the mountain fastnesses of Wales and Scotland, Anglo-Saxon writers would for the most part record the history of this turbulent century. Little wonder, then, so the conventional argument goes, that they chose to play down the role of the one British war leader who inflicted repeated defeats on them. Anglo-Saxon chroniclers are hardly going to make a song and dance about an enemy king who repeatedly defeated them. This is the major reason given for the absence of Arthur in contemporary records.

If you subscribe to this strictly propagandist view of history, that people will only record events which reflect favourably upon themselves, this explanation holds. Since Arthur beat the Saxons – albeit temporarily – they simply wrote him out of the story. True, there are plenty of examples throughout history of this happening but there are just as many examples of the opposite, of victors acknowledging the achievements of the vanquished. How much nobler to have overcome a powerful valiant enemy, than to have trounced a puny opposition. Some of the best evidence for Arthur's existence records that he defeated his enemies at least ten times, yet not a word of this is recorded by Saxon sources, nor is it even mentioned in Saxon sagas or poetry.

This situation is not eased by the fact that the only dated evidence we have for this period was not written by a Saxon but by a British monk called Gildas. Around AD 540, Gildas wrote a historical account of his times, *De Exidio et Conquestu Brittanniae* ('The Ruin and Fall of Britain'). Even though he was writing just twenty years after Arthur is supposed to have lived, and writing about that same period, there is no mention of Arthur, either as king or war leader.

It is clear from his own words that Gildas had an axe to grind. He was not pro-Saxon, but he was certainly anti-British. As a cleric he believed fervently that the Saxon invasion was a divine punishment – God exacting revenge on the lazy decadent Britons for their sins. His is a book aptly described by Alistair Moffat in *Arthur and the Lost Kingdoms*, as an account 'short on names and facts and long on blame and complaint'. Gildas certainly knew how to paint an apocalyptic picture of the fate of the British:

> All the greater towns fell to the enemy's battering rams; all their inhabitants, bishops, priests and people, were mown down together, while swords clashed and flames crackled. Horrible it was to see the foundation stones of towers and high walls thrown down bottom upward in the squares, mixing with holy altars and fragments of human bodies, as though they were covered with a crust of clotted blood, as in some fantastic wine-press. There was no burial in the ruins of the houses, only in the bellies of the beasts and birds.

Worse, Gildas talks of another British leader, Ambrosius Aurelianus, who revived the flagging fortunes of the nation in the face of the

Anglo-Saxon onslaught. Gildas states that Ambrosius was a brave soldier, better as a cavalryman than a foot soldier, then goes on to mention a great battle where the Saxons were defeated. He dates it precisely to AD 500, later known as the Battle of Mount Badon, but again he makes no mention of Arthur as the victor.

To do justice to our search, however, we must acknowledge that Gildas was a very bitter man, a man who reserved the very sharpest of his venom for the kings of Britain:

> Britain has kings, but they are tyrants . . . they often plunder and terrorise . . . the innocent; they defend and protect the guilty and the thieving; they have many wives . . . whores and adulteresses . . . they despise the harmless and the humble, but exalt to the stars, so far as they can, their military companions, bloody, proud and murderous men, adulterers and enemies of god . . . if chance, as they say, so allows: men who should be rooted out vigorously, name and all.

Hardly the image of our gallant chivalric hero Arthur – and, given his views on British kings in general, perhaps it is as well Gildas did not single out Arthur for special condemnation. More soberly, though, even given Gildas's special loathing for kings and general contempt for British leaders, it still seems incredible that he would not even mention a famous war leader just twenty years after he is said to have died. Could even an irascible old cleric, writing about Britain and the Second World War in the 1960s, fail to mention Winston Churchill? For me, the fact that Gildas makes no mention of Arthur is the strongest single piece of evidence that Arthur did *not* exist – at least not at that time.

A similar problem arises in AD 731 when a Northumbrian monk by the name of the Venerable Bede completed his *Ecclesiastical History of the English People*. Based at Jarrow in northern England, it is clear that his main concern was to document the Anglo-Saxon conquest of England. Bede relied heavily on Gildas for his account of the fifth century and skipped over the sixth century altogether. But, unlike Gildas, Bede is recognized as a gifted and generally accurate historian. So his total omission of Arthur as either king or war leader once again raises doubts about Arthur's existence during this period.

Better news comes from the early ninth-century Welsh monk known as Nennius, who is the first to name Arthur and provide us with some details of his life. However, this monk is alarmingly honest about his sources:

> I have heaped together all I have found, from the annals of the Romans, the chronicles of the Holy fathers, the writings of the Irish and the Saxons and the traditions of our own wise men.

So he declared his work to be a compilation of sources, ranging from historical records to fanciful legends ingeniously welded together into a chronological order. But at least here is Arthur on the page, doing battle against the invading Saxons.

Nennius is the first to depict Arthur not as a king (he gives his own king list elsewhere) but as a *Dux Bellorum*, a war leader who directs the battles in which British kings fought. He also introduces a magical element to Arthur, doubtless derived from the legendary sources he acknowledges using. In one incident, he recounts how 'the soldier Arthur's' dog left his paw print on a stone while chasing wild boar, and how subsequently Arthur built a cairn there to mark the miracle. In another, Nennius himself recounts visiting the tomb of one Anir, who was the soldier Arthur's son. This tomb magically changes size every time it is measured. But by far the most important section in Nennius details the soldier Arthur's campaign against the Saxons. This is such a vital passage that it is best to give it in full.

It was during this period that the war-leader Arthur, together with the kings of Britain, was fighting against the Saxons.

The first battle took place on the banks of the river Glein, while the second, third, fourth and fifth battles occurred beside another river, called the Dubglas, which is in the Linnius region. The sixth battle was on the river Bassus, and the seventh in the Celidon Wood, which is called 'Cat Coit Celidon'.

The eighth battle was at Castle Guinnion, where Arthur bore the image of the Holy Virgin Mary on his shoulders; on that day the pagans turned in flight and were slaughtered in great numbers, through the grace of Our Lord Jesus Christ and of his Holy Mother, the Virgin Mary.

The ninth battle was fought in the city of the legions (Caerlion), the tenth on the banks of a river called Tribuit, and the eleventh on a mountain called Agned. The twelfth was the battle at Mount Badon, in which nine hundred and sixty men were slain in a single charge by Arthur: all those were slain by Arthur himself, and he was victorious in every conflict.

Since they were defeated on each encounter, the Saxons sought help from Germany; they greatly increased their forces without interruption . . .

For the Arthur-seeker, these lines by Nennius are manna from heaven, providing wonderful clues for tracking down his military career. But, as with all things Arthurian, they prove to be a good deal more elusive than at first meets the eye. Of the twelve battle sites listed, only one has a certain location – Celidon Wood in southern Scotland, which is now called the Ettrick forest, lying just to the west of the town of Selkirk. It still covers a beautiful valley, a gushing stream tumbling down its centre, though much of the ancient wood has been either cleared for sheep-grazing or planted with conifer plantations. Fifteen hundred years ago, though, this wood was said to be the scene of a famous Arthurian battle, and Merlin was also said to have wandered through it, entirely mad.

Besides Celidon, Nennius does specify Caerlion as the 'city of the Legions', a famed, supposedly Arthurian site just outside the city of Newport in south Wales, just above the point where the river Usk flows into the Severn estuary. However, many scholars have assumed that Nennius – Welsh himself – added the parenthetical reference to the particular 'city of the Legions', so the original 'city of the Legions' might equally have been any one of the legionary bases in Britain.

As to the other sites, they are all either untraceable or ambiguous. There are, for example two rivers Glen (Glein), one in Lincolnshire and the other in Northumberland. Arguments have been put for both rivers as being the 'right' Arthurian one. The 'Dubglas' (Douglas) is even more problematic. The word means simply 'dark water' or 'black bog' in Celtic, and there are several rivers sporting that name in Britain. One of them is in Scotland, another in Lancashire, close to the major Roman garrison at Ribchester. Again, arguments have been made for both these rivers being the authentic source. Unfortunately nobody seems to have connected either of them with the 'Linnius' region.

There are several contenders for the river Tribuit, all of them essentially guesswork. The mouth of the river Severn is mooted, as is the estuary of the river Ribble in Lancashire. Castle Guinnion again appears to be anyone's guess. Even Mount Badon, the battle cited by Gildas, Bede, Nennius and the *Annals of Wales*, is of no certain fixed abode. Most people place it near Bath – and recent excavations have offered some support for this view – though whether we are talking about the low hills around the city of Bath or the ancient hill fort at Badbury Rings, near Swindon, is again open to conjecture. Just to make matters worse, it would be hard to argue honestly for any site in south-west England referred to as a 'Mount' rather than a hill.

So Nennius, tantalizingly concrete though he is, does not really get us any closer to the truth of who Arthur was or what he did and where.

The *Annals of Wales*, compilations of significant events according to the years they occurred, date to the late ninth or early tenth century, already some 400 years after Arthur may have lived. They tell of the Battle of Mount Badon and date it to AD 516. They also mention for the first time the battle where Arthur, along with his son Mordred, died. The oldest version does not make it clear if they died fighting against each other (as later legends have it) or side by side. A later version is clear, however:

> The battle of Camlam [also sometimes spelt Camblam and Cammlann], in which the famous Arthur, king of the British and Mordred his betrayer, fell by wounds inflicted by each other.

A few decades prior to the Welsh *Annals*, the Anglo-Saxons had completed their own chronicle which, like the Venerable Bede, aimed to record the progress of the Saxon conquest of Britain. It is the most comprehensive 'historical' document from this entire era. Dated to AD 870, it too makes no mention of Arthur as war lord or king. Most scholars, as already mentioned, consider this a case of airbrushing out an embarrassingly successful opponent, and I have already given my reasons for doubting such an assertion.

Arthur's next appearance is a few decades later, around AD 950, in the fable of Culhwch and Olwen, from the Welsh collection of stories known as the *Mabinogion*. Here there is no attempt to fit Arthur into history – we are firmly in the world of mythology. A certain Culhwch requests Arthur's help in securing the hand of Olwen, daughter of the Chief Giant, Ysbaddaden. We meet for the first time three of Arthur's most important knight-companions – Kay, Bedevere and Gawain. Arthur orders these three and sundry others to set off on a quest to help Culhwch secure his giantess, with consequences which anticipate many incidents in the later romances, in equally fanciful form.

Perhaps the importance of this early tale is that it gives us a glimpse of the likely rich oral tradition which had grown up around the figure of somebody called Arthur. Most of the fragments we have suggest that by this time Arthur was a familiar figure to the teller or listener of magical tales, and, just as is the case today, there was no need to introduce him because everybody knew who he was anyway.

From the beginning of the eleventh century, Arthur appears in a whole series of lives of saints, all written by Welsh clerics. Their attitude towards him is often ambivalent, however, as several of them clearly identify him as a secular, sometimes debauched ruler. This ambivalence may well be related to Gildas's loathing of the British kings. *The Life of St Goeznovius*, which is set in the opening decades of the new millennium around 1020, gives a brief Gildas-based sketch of early British history, followed by a very matter-of-fact account of Arthur. Here, though, a hint of immortality creeps into the portrait:

The pride of the Saxons was later suppressed by the great Arthur, King of the Britons, and they were driven from the greater part of the country and forced into servitude. However, when that same Arthur, after many splendid victories which he won in parts of Britain and Gaul, was recalled at length from worldly actions, the way was clear again for those Saxons who had remained in the island. Great oppression befell the British, and the Holy Church was persecuted.

Half a century later, around 1075, yet another Welsh cleric, Lifric of Llancarfan, brings Arthur into his *Life of St Cadoc*. Here, however, Lifric seems bent on sullying Arthur's reputation. First he has Arthur planning to abduct and rape the daughter of a defeated neighbouring king. Later, the saint and Arthur enter into dispute over compensation which Arthur demands for the killing of three of his knights. As a show of divine strength, just as the cows offered in compensation are being delivered, the saint turns them into bundles of ferns. Far from dumbstruck, however, Arthur immediately sets about the saintly conjuror with a whip. He then orders the saint into exile for seven years, seven months and seven days, before finally accepting the saint's prescription for the settling of the dispute.

This is the first rendering of a theme which recurs several times in ecclesiastical literature of the period. Here the 'recalcitrant king' is drawn away from tyranny down the path of righteousness by a pious saint. These are clearly moral tales, written by clerics with political ambitions, people who wish to assert the superior moral authority of spiritual leaders over their temporal counterparts. It was certainly the case that clerics did convert many ferocious battle-leaders during the Dark Ages, although we only have their word for it that they converted the British king Arthur.

Around 1100 Arthur has his first encounter with a dragon in *The Life of St Carannog*. Curiously though, it is not the mighty Arthur who takes on the beast; quite the contrary. The saint, coming to

Arthur's land by the banks of the river Severn, asks Arthur if he needs any favours done. Arthur tells the saint of a dragon which is laying waste to his fields. So the saint trots off, tames the dragon, brings it back to Arthur's citadel, and feeds it in front of the assembled, amazed masses. Naturally they try to kill it but the saint will not let them, pronouncing that the dragon was sent by God to destroy the sinners in the kingdom. Having thus gained all the moral high ground, the goodly saint then leads the puppy-dragon to the city gates and sends it away, telling it not to come back. Off it duly trots. Arthur is evidently so impressed that he gives the saint the keys to the city, and later makes him a grant of lands. Just the kind of pious ecclesiastical propaganda the church liked to promote, but of little help in our search for the historical Arthur.

A much more interesting reference appears in William of Malmesbury's *Deeds of the English Kings* from around AD 1125. He accepts Nennius's account of the Battle of Mount Badon, although he considered Arthur to be war leader to Ambrosius (who is generally cast as Arthur's uncle), not king. But his revealing comments concern the way Arthur is held in twelfth-century folk memory:

> They [the Britons] would have been totally destroyed had not Ambrosius . . . repressed the swelling hordes of barbarians through the distinguished achievements of the warlike Arthur.
>
> It is about this Arthur that the Britons tell such trifling stories even today. Clearly, he is a man more worthy to be extolled in true histories, as the leader who preserved his tottering homeland and kindled an appetite for war in the shattered minds of his countrymen, than to be dreamed of in fallacious fables.

In a further reference to folk tales William touches on the theme of the 'Once and Future King':

The tomb of Arthur is nowhere to be found, for which reason ancient fables claim that he will return again.

Although these references are brief, they are admirably clear and make it certain that Arthur was an important legendary figure who had not been forgotten, at least not among the British, by the twelfth century.

Later that century, Caradoc of Llancarfan decided to write a biography of his great hero – none other than St Gildas, who had ignored Arthur 500 years before. Caradoc had figured out that Gildas and Arthur must have been contemporaries. In a glorious conceit, he informs his readers that Gildas's eldest brother was a warrior called Hueil. This is what happens:

Hueil, a habitual warrior and a most famous soldier, refused to obey any king, even Arthur. He used to harass Arthur, and they provoked each other with the greatest fury. Hueil invaded from Scotland on many occasions, setting fire to the land and bearing off booty with victory and praise.

For this reason Arthur, king of all Britain, hearing of the achievements of this brave, excellent and most victorious youth, felt oppressed, since the native people said and hoped that he would be their future king. So, by fierce persecution and in open warfare, Arthur killed the young pillager on the Isle of Minau.

Caradoc was putting out the rumour that Gildas had excluded Arthur from his seminal work because the warrior-king had killed his brother. This idea rapidly gained currency at an interesting time – the time when the greatest account of Arthur's life was being greeted with popular acclaim. In 1136, Geoffrey of Monmouth, yet another

Welsh cleric, swept aside all of the Welsh church's snide side-swiping at Arthur and proclaimed him the most noble lost hero and true founder of the British nation. There were good political reasons for Geoffrey doing this, but to get to these we first need to backtrack over the known history of the preceding 300 years.

Despite their best efforts the Britons had lost control of most of England by the end of the seventh century AD. This is not to say that they had been exterminated, but they had certainly been dominated and absorbed by the Anglo-Saxons. Independent, Celtic-speaking Britons were confined to Wales, Cornwall and some pockets of Scotland, and they were of course in touch with the Celtic-speaking communities in Ireland and Brittany. Over the following centuries, the Saxon settlements in eastern England were repeatedly raided by Danish and Norse peoples, some of whom stayed and became absorbed into the Anglo-Saxon polity. Although Norse influences can be found in Old English, it seems that the tongue remained predominantly Anglo-Saxon. By the beginning of the eleventh century, the people thought of themselves as English, although the Britons and many foreigners called them Saxons.

William the Conqueror, arriving in 1066, was the illegitimate son of a Norman duke – a man of Norse or Viking descent who had settled in northern France. 'Norman' is an abbreviation of 'Norse-man'. As a mere duke, William was a vassal to the King of France and could only claim the English throne on behalf of the French king. However, William maintained that his mother was a Breton and in fact a direct descendant of the great king Arthur. William therefore used his mother's 'royal' bloodline as the basis for his claim to the British throne.

The Normans were extremely vicious in their suppression of the Anglo-Saxon population of England, but their aim was domination, not extermination. They needed the Saxons to be their villeins (serfs), to plough the land, build their castles and churches, and to fight their wars. They quickly eliminated the Saxon aristocracy and parcelled out the land to their own kinsmen, but they never succeeded in replacing the English tongue with French, their own adopted language. (French was the language of the court and of all authority for more than 200 years and much of it seeped into the vernacular, but the people stubbornly refused to accept it.)

Perhaps by the beginning of the twelfth century, the ruling élite, aware that they would never be able to impose their own language and culture on the people, were looking for a new way of denigrating Saxon culture while ennobling their own. Either way, with the publication of Geoffrey of Monmouth's account of Arthur, a way fell open to pursue their legitimacy through William's other bloodline. In this tale, the heroes were William's ancestors and the villains were certainly Saxons.

I rather suspect that Geoffrey had not intended his book to be anything more than the retelling of a piece of history which had mostly languished in Welsh oral tradition for several centuries, but when it dovetailed so neatly with the political desires of the ruling élite, it was guaranteed to be a best-seller.

Perhaps I am being too charitable to Geoffrey. He was certainly a wily old fox. For a start, his story concerns an illegitimate son (Arthur) who becomes a conquering hero and king, just as William the Conqueror (also a bastard) was known to be. And who does Geoffrey dedicate his book to? Why, to Robert, Earl of Gloucester, illegitimate son of King Henry I. And he passes the buck of authenticity very neatly in the second paragraph of the preface where he tells us:

... Walter, Archdeacon of Oxford ... presented me with a certain very ancient book written in the British language. This book, attractively composed to form a consecutive and orderly narrative, set out all the deeds of those men, from Brutus, the first king of the Britons, down to Cadwallader, son of Cadwallo. At Walter's request I have taken the trouble to translate the book into Latin . . .

Geoffrey's source-book has never seen the light of day, nor do other references exist to a history of the kings of Britain written in British. This is a manuscript which mysteriously appears then disappears at the beck and call of its 'translator'. So while we can't prove that this vital source did not exist, we certainly have no evidence that it did.

Whatever his sources for the *The History of the Kings of Britain*, Geoffrey's account of Arthur is qualitatively different from all the earlier sources in that it is very long, very comprehensive, and, as he himself says, 'a story'. In this sense, Geoffrey's work is rightly seen as the foundation stone of the flood of Arthurian tales which followed – the works which make up the Arthurian canon, culminating in the *Vulgate Cycle* in France and Malory's *Le Morte D'Arthur* in England. As a work purporting to be fact it was hammered, even by Geoffrey's peers. Writing just forty years after Geoffrey's death, chronicler William of Newburgh condemned the book utterly:

> It is quite clear that everything this man wrote about Arthur and his successors, or indeed about his predecessors from Vortigern onwards, was made up, partly by himself and partly by others, either from an inordinate love of lying, or for the sake of pleasing the Britons.

We must not wholly condemn Geoffrey, however, for the importance of his work is far better judged in terms of its pivotal role in the development of the Arthurian canon. Lewis Thorpe, writing in the Introduction to the Penguin edition of Geoffrey's book, hits the right note:

> Whatever curious elements of truth the book might contain, Geoffrey of Monmouth's 'History of the Kings of Britain' was, as we have seen, severely criticised by more orthodox historians writing well within the author's own century. As romanticised history on the other hand, as a source book for the imaginative writing of others, as an inspiration for poetry, drama and romantic fiction down the centuries, it has few if any equals in the whole history of European literature.

Geoffrey's role in the birth of Arthurian romantic literature is an indisputable fact, but whether his story contains verifiable grains of truth is a much more problematic question. To give his story the feel of authenticity, Geoffrey plants his characters and actions firmly in the known landscape of the British Isles, and in some parts of Europe. By so doing, he set in train 'Arthurian associations' which are still very much alive today. Often because of these associations, several of the key sites have been subject to archaeological investigation to determine if there was any truth in his tales.

Geoffrey has Arthur conceived at the royal castle of Tintagel, on the north Cornish coast. Merlin temporarily transforms Arthur's father Uther Pendragon into the likeness of Gorlois, Duke of Cornwall, so that he can seduce Ygerna, the duke's wife. The ruse works and Arthur the bastard is conceived. This is certainly a colourful and expedient start to the royal tale, but it hardly rings of historical truth. Yet the connection of the site with Arthur has stuck. In part this must be because of the mysterious nature of Tintagel. A deep cove cuts into the jagged cliffs on two sides of what is all but an island. A narrow strip of land, originally bridged, joins this promontory to the mainland. The sea crashes into the shoreline constantly, filling the air with the roars of the surge and salty spray. Caves, including one known as Merlin's cave, produce weird echoes as the sea runs deep into them. Some caverns run clean under a headland, from cove to cove.

With eyes averted from the tourist sprawl at the top of the cliffs, this place certainly has a magical ring about it. The island would have been virtually impregnable once its entrance was fortified, and the area it encloses is much larger than the familiar aerial photographs suggest. There was certainly ample space for housing and grazing. If a water supply could be secured, anyone could withstand a siege there almost indefinitely.

In Geoffrey's time there was no castle there but it already had a reputation as a noble, even royal residence. This has been borne out by recent excavations, which have revealed that the site was occupied during the Roman and post-Roman period, and was also an extremely important centre for international trade. Debris from the excavation layers corresponding to the fifth and sixth centuries – Arthur's days – contain a huge number of fragments of imported ceramics, mostly wine and oil jars originating from the eastern Mediterranean. In fact, the recent excavations have revealed more of these fragments there than have been found in the rest of Britain and Ireland. Other finds have demonstrated direct trade links between Spain and Britain in the fifth century, establishing beyond doubt that Tintagel was a major trade centre, dealing in luxury items used exclusively by noble or royal families.

Although the bay is quite well sheltered and anchorage would have been relatively easy, Tintagel is not an ideal harbour. There are many better places in the south-west, the Falmouth estuary being just one obvious example. So it seems that trade was being drawn to this spot by a special magnet, which was probably the presence of powerful noble patrons there.

Tintagel made the front pages in August 1998, when a team of archaeologists working there revealed that they had unearthed a slate drain-cover with a word something like 'Arthur' scratched on it. The drain-cover was from the right period and had in fact been some sort of wall plaque before being broken and placed over the drain. It actually has two inscriptions on it, the more lightly inscribed reading *PATER/COLI AVI FICIT/ARTOGNOV*. This apparently means 'Artognou, father of a descendant of Col, has had this made/built/ constructed'.

Inevitably, the Press leapt at this 'proof' of Arthur's presence at Tintagel. Enthusiasts were also quick to associate the name Col with the Coel Hen (the original Old King Cole), a documented king of northern Britain who may also have been a war leader. Fortunately the director of the excavation team, Chris Morris from the University of Glasgow, is not the type of person to be dragged along by media speculation. While agreeing that the first part of the name, 'Art' uses the Celtic element *artos*, meaning bear, he is categorical that the second part does not render it Arthur. As Morris puts it:

> There has been much media speculation about the inscription, but suffice it to say that it does NOT read as 'Arthur'. We must dismiss any idea that the name on this stone is in any way connected with that legendary and literary figure.

A pity really, as this near-miss is by far the closest anyone has ever come to a positive identification of a genuine Arthurian remain.

Geoffrey of Monmouth also sets some of his action in Dimilioc fort, just five miles from Tintagel. This is an ancient earthen rampart and ditch fort, although it has no known connections with the period. He sites Arthur's last fatal battle of Camblam (most subsequent scholars call it Camlann) hard by Tintagel, at Camelford. Once again local folklore concurs with this, and the bridge over the river Camel is called Slaughter Bridge. But there is no concrete evidence of any battle having been fought there in the post-Roman period.

A string of Roman locations are also used by Geoffrey – York, one of the several Cities of the Legions, as well as Caerleon in south Wales, another important Roman military centre. Bath, with its Roman spa, is the setting for the Battle of Mount Badon and Lincoln is also mentioned. Like everyone else, Geoffrey puts Caledon Wood in Scotland – and more action is set in unspecified parts of Scotland. Other action takes place in Somerset, and Geoffrey is the first to dispatch the dying Arthur to the Island of Avalon, widely held to be Glastonbury Tor, towering over the marshy lakeland of the Somerset Levels before they were drained.

Here is the home of yet another intriguing little Arthurian hoax. Glastonbury had been a religious centre and pilgrimage site since the seventh century, but in 1174 a fire destroyed part of the abbey and many of the saintly relics which attracted pilgrims. King Henry II sent funds for restoring the building, but the Abbey's prestige and revenue were severely damaged. Then in 1191 the monks announced a miraculous 'discovery'. While digging a grave for a fellow monk, they claimed they had stumbled upon a tomb containing three coffins. There was also a cross inscribed in ancient Latin announcing that there lay the body of the famous king Arthur, buried in the Isle of Avalon.

Initially the monks announced that the bodies were Arthur, Guinevere and Mordred, but they rapidly changed their story and lost Mordred's coffin when the idea that Arthur would have been buried with the son who betrayed him was ridiculed. The cross disappeared in the seventeenth century, though not before it had been sketched by an antiquarian named William Camden. Although an attempt has been made to make the lettering look authentic, the orthography is not of the sixth century, nor is the fact that Arthur is referred to as 'king'. Outside the sanctified walls of Glastonbury Abbey, this charade has long been accepted as a fraud in the old monkish tradition of 'discovering' holy relics.

In a similar vein, Arthur's famous Round Table has hung on the walls of Winchester Great Hall since 'time immemorial', but because it is made of wood it was easy to date once Carbon 14 dating techniques were developed in the 1940s. Alas, it was fashioned in the thirteenth century, proving it to be another little Arthurian peccadillo, this time perpetrated by the good people of Winchester.

As the Arthurian legends developed, a steady stream of new sites and characters – some real, some imaginary – were added to the geography of Arthurian Britain. Around 1177, the great French romancer Chrétien de Troyes introduced both Lancelot, the (French) finest knight in all Christendom, and Camelot, although he does not tell us where it was. And by the time Caxton was preparing the preface for Malory's *Le Morte D'Arthur* in 1485, the defendant of Arthur was listing Glastonbury (Arthur's tomb), the tomb of Edward the Confessor in Westminster Abbey (Arthur's seal in red wax), Dover Castle (Gawain's skull), Winchester (the Round Table), the town of Camelot in Wales (great stones and marvellous works of iron lying under the ground), and 'other places' where Lancelot's sword and many other relics were to be found. In the text itself, Malory maintains that Stonehenge was built from stones which Merlin had carried from Ireland and set up himself on Salisbury Plain. A charming idea, but not one borne out by archaeology.

This game of discovering Arthurian sites continues down the centuries, and is currently enjoying a formidable renaissance. In the last eight years at least six books have appeared, all purporting to trace the home and life story of the 'real' Arthur. Every one of them relies heavily on the art of toponymy, tracing Arthurian links in the naming of the landscape. Three of them find Arthur, Camelot and his battle sites concentrated in Wales. The fourth locates him in the West Midlands with links into central Wales. The fifth follows the conventional (and least convincing) route and finds him in south-west England. The sixth book is the most plausible and finds him battling against Picts and invading Saxons, in the Scottish border-lands, from a base at a site now known as Roxburgh Castle.

It should come as little surprise that the majority of these authors find Arthur on their home turf – the Welsh find him in Wales, the Scots in the Borders, the English in the Midlands and the south-west of England. I am told that this phenomenon of the 'local Arthur' is even more widespread. Apparently there are local Arthurian histori-cal societies, scattered all over the country, which have worked out their own 'maps' of the Arthurian adventures in much the same way that Alistair Moffat has found him in Scotland and Alan Wilson and Baram Blackett have found him in Wales.

I do not find this particularly surprising. It is very clear even from this brief survey of historical sources that stories about Arthur were in wide circulation for centuries – but were also essentially vague in terms of precise time and place. Mythology is like that – if it is not, then it is history. It also tends to be 'domesticated' by its proponents – myth-tellers like to associate the stories they tell with local landscapes.

I had first-hand experience of this 'mythical map' syndrome when working with non-literate people in the Amazon forests. I discovered there that, once I had got the hang of a particular myth, I could travel 50 or 100 miles away and hear exactly the same story told, with totally different geographical details. So, while in one village, Old Thunder Man lived under the deep (and real) Caruru waterfall, according to another story-teller – living near the Jaguar waterfalls – the same Old Thunder Man lived there, and so on.

Oral tradition likes nothing better than to blend itself into the local landscape, to give the tellers and hearers the eerie sense that, 'once upon a time and long ago', these amazing things actually happened right under their noses. By doing this, we infuse both the stories and the local landscape with a mystical charge which makes us tingle at the thought that here there once really were ... dragons!

This process has undoubtedly taken place over much of Britain in relation to Arthur. There are multiple contenders for almost all the major 'locations' in the tales and, in all, more than 2000 extant place-names which are said to relate to the Arthurian legends. In my view, then, the discovery of a 'match' between local place-names and the events in a narrative is evidence of *mythic* maps, not historical ones.

Overall, it seems to me that the evidence for the existence of a historical figure called Arthur, at the end of the fifth and beginning of the sixth century, is extremely thin. Innumerable writers have found him there because they wanted to, *not* because evidence exists to support their case. If Arthur had not been perceived from so early on as such a key figure in the formation of the British national identity, then I doubt that anyone would have given Nennius's assertions a second glance. The total lack of support for his existence in the archaeological record further endorses my suspicion that Arthur is in essence a mysterious and mythical character.

I hope it is clear from the evidence presented in this chapter that a great deal of guile has been used in the manufacture of the Arthurian story. Nennius, honest enough to admit that he is only working from scraps and fragments, is smart enough to realize that if he has Arthur fighting as war leader *with* the kings of England, then he need not contradict the established sixth-century king lists, which of course do not mention a king Arthur.

In fact, the very name Arthur is pretty rare in the period under discussion. Several writers have claimed that there was an increase in the use of the name in noble and royal families in the second half of the sixth century – and they suggest that this '*in memoriam*' usage is corroborative evidence that a great man must have borne that name earlier in the century (rather like the rash of 'Dianas' which followed the marriage of the late Princess of Wales), but this can hardly be seen as proof of his existence.

Yet, by the time the Arthurian tales start to appear in any detail in print – some 500 years later – the 'mighty shadow' is treated with a familiarity and solidity which seems to take his historical veracity for granted. At the same time, right from the start, the Arthurian tales were loaded with a wealth of detail about the behaviour and culture of the protagonists which cannot be placed safely in the British sixth-century context.

So, before we attempt to trace the origins of all these exotic ideas and events, we need to take a close look at the Arthurian literature, generated principally in England and France between AD 1136 and 1485.

CHAPTER FOUR

Dreams of Arthur

Medieval Literature

ALTHOUGH GEOFFREY OF MONMOUTH CLAIMED THAT HIS WORK, THE first coherent account of the life of king Arthur, was historically accurate, we have seen that this is not the case. But his book did generate the framework, the narrative structure which underpins virtually all of the subsequent outpouring of Arthurian literature over the following 350 years.

This vast body of medieval literature came into being in three possible ways: firstly (and most commonly) the tales, or parts of the tales, were elaborations of the basic ideas and motifs laid down by Geoffrey and his predecessors. Secondly, pre-existing folk tales were modified to incorporate Arthurian characters or reset within the overall Arthurian scheme of things. This latter process probably accounts for the vast body of literature relating to the quest for the Holy Grail, unmentioned by Geoffrey and his predecessors, in which Arthur is a marginal character excluded from the central action. Thirdly, some of the medieval Arthurian material may have been pure fiction – the product of each author's imagination.

In most cases, at least two of the three creative processes were combined to produce new works. For example, the 'sword in the stone' motif (absent from Geoffrey's work) was very probably plucked from a different folk tale and welded imaginatively into the Arthurian canon by Malory. In all cases, though, the question is not one of historical accuracy; as we examine the medieval literature we are firmly in the realms of romantic fiction, albeit glossed with a historical veneer.

Much of the development and elaboration of the Arthurian tales took place in France in the twelfth and thirteenth centuries; in particular the creation of the character of Lancelot and his adulterous adoration of Guinevere has French origins, in the writings of Chrétien de Troyes. The notion of the Grail Quest also originates with Chrétien, who introduces us to many new knights who undertake the quest. That it is a Frenchman – Lancelot's son Galahad – who finally achieves the Grail, strongly suggests that these aspects of the legends are intended to give the French a large share of the action, relegating Arthur to the role of a cuckolded, incompetent ruler.

As mentioned in Chapter Three, the French versions culminate in the last book of the *Vulgate Cycle*, 'The Death of Arthur', a magnificently lean, action-packed rendering of a story which has at its centre the doomed love of Lancelot for Guinevere, and decidedly not the glories of king Arthur.

Perhaps it was this blatant hijacking of the British hero and his subversion at the hands of the French romancers which led Caxton and Malory to produce the final and definitive medieval form of the Arthurian tales. By calling it *Le Morte D'Arthur* they trumpeted its French origins, but in their mammoth rendition in 1485 subtly altered the balance back in favour of Arthur.

This same year saw the Battle of Bosworth and the coming of the Tudor dynasty to the British throne, marking, in many ways, the end of the medieval era in Britain. Nothing stood so quintessentially for this period than the Arthurian legends portrayed at their most elaborate by Caxton and Malory. Their enrichment was in part due to the changing fashions of the mid and late Middle Ages. It was also the result of the accretion of new characters and actions to the stories. These 'new' aspects of the tales were in most cases 'borrowings' from other folk tales and oral traditions. It is clear, though, that throughout this long evolutionary period nothing was added as a result of factual verifiable discoveries.

Geoffrey of Monmouth's *The History of the Kings of Britain* (1136) has a certain authentic ring about it, mostly because it was written before the days of high chivalry characteristic of the later books. The pages are not cluttered with endless knights questing and jousting for the favour of fair damsels. Instead the struggle to form and maintain alliances – or to gain the upper hand in battle – are to the fore. The avowed 'historical' intent of Geoffrey's narrative is to reveal the heroic course of Arthur's victories on the British and European stage, and to tell the story of a glorious king, not to get bogged down in court intrigues, adultery and deception.

There is no doubt that Geoffrey's work maps out the basics of the Arthurian biography. But his book is almost as interesting for what it does *not* contain as for what is there. Many of the most basic elements we would expect to find are absent – Camelot, the sword in the stone and Lancelot – are just three examples. If you read it in this way, it is clearly the starting point of a story which positively invites elaboration.

Interestingly, though, because Geoffrey is purporting to write a full and authentic account of the history of *all* the kings of Britain, he starts the Arthurian tale much earlier than later writers. He introduces Merlin to his readers long before Arthur is on the scene. His Merlin is a child due to be sacrificed by Vortigern (the British leader who first invited in the Saxons). The boy will die to consecrate a site where Vortigern has been trying unsuccessfully to build a castle – every time he puts up walls they shake and collapse. The fearless boy Merlin claims he can solve the problem and orders Vortigern's men to dig a big pit on the site, prophesying that at the bottom they will find a pool with two stones in it. These, he says, contain sleeping dragons.

With the pit dug and the pool duly drained, Vortigern sits down on the banks of the pool. Soon two dragons emerge, one red, one white. Seeing one another they immediately fight, spitting fire. The white dragon drives the red one to the edge of the pool who in turn drives the white dragon back to the centre. As the battle rages, Vortigern asks the boy-sorcerer Merlin to explain. Entering a prophetic trance Merlin names the red dragon as the Britons (hence the Welsh national flag) and the white dragon the Saxons. He prophesies that the white dragon would be in the ascendant and would drive the red dragon back and back. A long list of apocalyptic prophecies follows (Geoffrey was evidently keen on Merlin's prophecies and wrote a separate book of them), predicting the ruin and fall of the British state.

Somewhat later, a fiery dragon appears in the sky. This time Merlin is summoned by Uther, the ruling king's brother. Merlin's interpretation is that the king (who is elsewhere) has died and the fiery celestial dragon is an omen that Uther will be a great leader. This, according to Geoffrey, is how Uther came to be called Uther *Pendragon*, 'Dragon's Head'. Merlin also points to a dazzling ray of light emanating from the dragon and says that it represents Uther's (unborn) son, who will be a super-powerful man.

A short time after, we reach the point where most of the later literature begins. Uther Pendragon lusts after the Duke of Cornwall's wife and persuades Merlin to help him to impregnate her. In Geoffrey's version the cuckolded duke is then killed and his wife Ygerna taken by Uther. They have two children, Arthur and Anna, who are reared in court. In later versions Merlin demands that Uther give up the baby Arthur to his keeping until it is time for him to become king.

In Geoffrey's story, Uther Pendragon gradually ages and, after defeating the Saxons, expires. His bastard son Arthur gains the throne aged fifteen. There is no magic about this process, no sword in the stone, no sudden appearance under Merlin's wing, no crowd of jealous British lords and kings conspiring his demise. Instead Arthur gathers up his followers and does battle with the Saxons on the banks of the river Douglas, then lays siege to them at York (as per Nennius's battle history). A series of further battles ensue, again following the Nennius prescription, culminating in the Battle of Mount Badon.

Some interesting lines precede this battle. Geoffrey arms Arthur:

Arthur himself put on a leather jerkin worthy of so great a king. On his head he placed a golden helmet with a crest carved in the shape of a dragon; and across his shoulders a shield called Pridwen on which was painted the likeness of the Blessed Mary, mother of God, . . . He girded on his peerless sword Caliburn, which was forged in the Isle of Avalon. A spear called Ron graced his right hand: long, broad in the blade and thirsty for slaughter.

In the battle itself Arthur turns the tide with a massive personal hit-rate, although Geoffrey only accords him 470 victims, as against 960 in Nennius's head-count.

Having sorted out the Scots and Picts up in Scotland, Arthur then decides to marry Guinevere (mentioned here for the first time). As one would expect, she is the most beautiful woman in the land, but a descendant of a noble Roman family brought up by the Duke of Cornwall, not the independent queen of the Summer Country as she would later become.

Arthur then sets off almost immediately on a tour of alliance-building and conquest all over north-west Europe, from France to Iceland to Norway and Denmark. Turning his attention to Gaul, he finds himself in single combat with the Roman tribune Frollo. The duel is fought exactly as at a tourney, with a single lance-charge as openers followed by swordplay on the ground, which Arthur duly wins. Once Gaul is subdued and the rule of law established, Arthur gives the province of Normandy to his cup-bearer Bedevere, and Anjou to his seneschal (steward) Kay.

Returning to Britain, Arthur decides to hold a splendid coronation at the City of the Legions (Caerleon) in south Wales. Dignitaries come from all over the world, and are showered with gifts by Arthur, who is renowned for his generosity. The pageant culminates in all manner of games 'competed on horseback ... without the slightest show of ill-feeling'. However, at the end of the celebrations, an envoy arrives with a letter from the Roman Emperor, demanding tribute. Arthur and his guest fellow-rulers decide not to brook this imperial cheek – and declare war on Rome. An immense army assembles – the British mostly cavalry, the people from the other islands mostly infantry.

Aboard ship on his way to do battle on mainland Europe, Arthur falls into a deep sleep. He dreams of a bear flying through the air, then sees a terrifying dragon flying in from the west and lighting up the countryside with the glare of its eyes.

The dragon and bear fight, and the dragon is victorious. When Arthur wakes and relates his dream, his companions are certain that he has dreamt of his own victory. So even though we know that the 'Art' of Arthur means 'bear' in Celtic, Geoffrey – a Welsh-speaker – still makes the dragon Arthur's mystical manifestation.

A curious incident follows. Arthur decides to destroy a giant who has abducted a fair damsel and is holding her at Mont-Saint-Michel in Brittany. After a Titanic struggle, Arthur slays the giant with Caliburn. He then orders Bedevere to saw off the giant's head and carry it back to camp for all to see. Arthur recalls that he has not done battle with anyone so strong since he killed the giant Retho:

> Retho had made himself a fur cloak from the beards of the kings he had slain . . .

After killing the giant, Arthur takes the trophy beard-cloak and adds the giant's beard to it. He now has his own kings' beards' cloak.

Geoffrey then moves Arthur on to the scene of the climactic battle with the Roman legions, setting it near the river Aube in the vicinity of what is now the town of Troyes. An epic tussle begins, with Arthur commanding from his royal standard, the Golden Dragon, while the Romans rally to the Imperial standard, the Golden Eagle. Arthur exhorts his men to victory and promises them that after the battle:

> . . . we can set off for Rome itself . . . When we have occupied

it . . . and yours shall be its gold, silver, palaces, towers, castles, cities and all the other riches of the vanquished!

The battle goes this way and that, with the Romans deploying superior numbers of infantry in wedge-shaped formations against a mixed force of British–Gallic cavalry and infantry. Cavalry charges repeatedly break the Roman lines and cavalry pursuits are deadly at cutting down the fleeing enemy. Bedevere is killed, and Kay mortally wounded by the Medes (Persians) and Libyans fighting for the Romans. He makes his way back to Arthur's royal standard with Bedevere's body. Bedevere's nephew, Hyrelgas, incensed by his uncle's death, spearheads a cavalry charge straight into the ranks of the Medes – 'for all the world like a wild boar through a pack of hounds' – and, succeeding in killing the King of the Medes, carries his body back, putting it down next to his uncle's body, then hacks it to pieces.

The battle rages on, with much slaughter on both sides. The Romans seem to be getting the upper hand until they come face to face with Arthur's personal command. Drawing his sword ready to counter-attack, Geoffrey's description pulls no punches in glorifying his hero's martial prowess:

Arthur dashed straight at the enemy. He flung them to the ground and cut them to pieces. Whoever came his way was either killed himself or had his horse killed under him at a single blow. They ran away from him as sheep run from a fierce lion whom raging hunger compels to devour all that chance throws in his way. Their armour offered them no protection capable of preventing Caliburn, when wielded in the right hand of this mighty King, from forcing them to vomit forth their souls with their life-blood. Ill luck brought two kings, Sertorious of Libya and Politetes of Bithynia, in Arthur's way. He hacked off their heads and bundled them off to hell.

Victory inevitably falls to Arthur, who spends the rest of the year consolidating his position in France. The following summer he is about to set off to sack Rome when news reaches him that his British throne has been usurped by his nephew Mordred (in later versions, Mordred is said to be Arthur's son from his incestuous relationship with his sister) and that:

> this treacherous tyrant was living adulterously and out of wedlock with Guinevere, who had broken the vows of her earlier marriage.

Here Geoffrey coyly breaks off the narrative, sensing he is on prickly ground when it comes to royal adulterous incest. He addresses his (bastard) royal patron directly:

> About this particular matter, most noble Duke, Geoffrey of Monmouth prefers to say nothing. He will, however . . . describe the battle which our most famous king fought against his nephew, once he had returned to Britain after his victory; for he had found it in the British treatise already referred to. He heard it, too, from Walter of Oxford, a man most learned in all branches of history.

Cautious once again to assure us of the authenticity of his tale – and careful also to pass the buck to Walter of Oxford – Geoffrey finishes the story with a battle as Arthur is landing in England (in which Gawain is killed), Arthur's riposte and pursuit of Mordred, then the final battle of Camblam (following the *Annals of Wales*, although with a different date), in which 'the accursed traitor' Mordred is killed and:

> Arthur himself, our renowned King, was mortally wounded and was carried off to the Isle of Avalon, so that his wounds might be attended to. He handed the crown of Britain over to his cousin Constantine, the son of the Duke of Cornwall: this in the year 542 after our Lord's incarnation.

So Geoffrey's tale ends, without Arthur officially dead and buried, but also with no mention of Ladies of the Lake, hands grasping Caliburn, golden barques with three queens aboard, and only the ambiguity of Arthur carried off to Avalon to have his wounds tended, hinting at the 'Once and Future King'.

Briefly, we should first establish that this entire tale has no more basis in historical truth than the writings of Nennius. The events which Geoffrey purports to chronicle – Arthur's victories over the Romans, his establishment of an immense empire, from Iceland to Italy, his battles with his treacherous son/nephew, and so on – are either absolutely unverifiable or demonstrably false. There are no traces of British invasions of any of the places mentioned, either in the archaeological record or in written texts. The various kings, Roman tribunes and emperors he evokes are all either incorrect or wrongly dated. I have already established that the famed battles with the Saxons, derived directly from Nennius's list, are of very dubious authenticity. This is historical fiction, not fact.

But it is *historical* fiction (or perhaps we should say chronological or narrative fiction). Geoffrey's genius is that his story is for the most part so well portrayed that it seems plausible. Here we have Arthur, a heroic figure, attaining dizzy heights, retaining them through valour and martial skills, facing and defeating overwhelming odds, then being dragged into a mighty fall, a tragic and mysterious end. It is such a good story that it remains intact for 350 years – Malory's twenty-one-book version uses virtually everything contained in Geoffrey's work, although almost all the incidents are embellished in some way or another and a great deal of extra material is added.

But besides forging the pseudo-historical narrative form of the Arthur story, Geoffrey also introduces a decidedly weird mystical twist to his tale-telling. Doubtless derived from folklore and oral tradition, there are a series of incidents which clearly carry a sufficiently powerful mythic 'charge' that Geoffrey determines to include them despite their obvious absurdity in pragmatic historical terms. We should not forget that from Geoffrey's point of view he is writing about ancient history in 1136, just as I am writing about ancient history today. He too felt he was writing about the mists of time, unveiling hidden lost truths from the days when dragons and giants walked the earth. I find it very intriguing that it is precisely this mystical aspect of his tales which the later writers choose to embroider even more than the fantastical-historical aspects.

The first of these mystical events arises when the boy Merlin, chosen as a sacrificial victim, reveals the fighting dragons to Vortigern. This is followed by the appearance of a fiery dragon in the sky which gives Arthur's father his epithet and foretells of Arthur's arrival. There are so many references in early literature all round the world to ominous fiery beasts in the sky that it is safe to assume that they derive from comets and asteroid showers. None the less, it is interesting that in both its autochthonous and celestial forms the dragon is firmly associated with prophecy – the ability to see the future.

This, however, is not how dragons were portrayed in Celtic societies of classical and post-Roman times. Throughout this period, dragons were treated in folk tradition as yet another essentially threatening beast which needed to be overcome by a conquering hero like Arthur or St George. There is no evidence to support the idea that a dragon might be a positive beneficial force allied to powerful people in British or Gallic tradition. Yet it is very clear that by the time Geoffrey was writing, the dragon had undergone this transformation in the folk psyche. In the eleventh century, the dragon represented not only the Cymry, the British people of Wales, but the Scottish nation too. It remained a dominant national symbol right down to the sixteenth century, where it was retained as a part of the royal coat of arms, reflecting Henry Tudor's Welsh origins.

To bring the dragon's prophecy to fruition, Merlin uses magic potions to turn Uther temporarily into the Duke of Cornwall. This ability to turn one thing or person into another has been part of the sorcerer's required skills since ancient days, and recurs several times in the later Arthurian canon.

Magic is also conjured when it comes to Arthur's weaponry. He has clearly taken the symbol of the golden dragon to his heart and places it on both his helmet and his battle standard. His sword, Caliburn, has magical powers and hails from the paradisiacal Island of Avalon – a place of regeneration as symbolized by apple orchards. To play it safe, Geoffrey tags along with Nennius and gives Arthur a shield with a Christian symbol on it, but he also gives him a magic spear with the slightly incongruous name 'Ron'.

The supernatural origins of Geoffrey's magical armoury are, however, kept vague, and this is an area where later writers excel in elaboration and diversification. By the time we reach Malory there are two incidents of swords in stones (Arthur's and Galahad's). Arthur has two different swords, one non-magic pulled from the stone, the other Excalibur presented to him by the Lady of the Lake. Excalibur is important because it makes its holder invincible, but Merlin instructs Arthur that its scabbard is even more important as its wearer cannot lose blood from wounds. Various incidents in Malory's books revolve around the thefts of both the sword and its scabbard. The return of Excalibur to the Lady of the Lake becomes the climactic moment in the Arthurian finale, although it is clearly a post-Geoffrey accretion.

Dreaming as a means of access to Otherworld knowledge – and as prophecy in symbolic form – only occurs once in Geoffrey, but is used several times in later versions. I have already mentioned the slight anomaly in Arthur dreaming of a battle between the dragon (him) and the bear (Rome, but also the root of his name). This is neatly circumvented by Malory, where Arthur dreams of a conflict between the dragon (self) and a wild boar (popular Saxon symbol).

Shortly after the dream aboard ship bound for France, Arthur takes on the giant at Mont-Saint-Michel. This is a mystical although pretty routine undertaking in legendary terms. Biblical, classical, Irish, Welsh, Norse – and almost all other myth cycles – abound with heroes laying out giants. Cutting off their heads to display one's prowess is also a fairly standard ploy. After all, it is that much more glorious to defeat a large person than an ordinary fellow mortal. But the curious thing about this episode is what it reminds Arthur of. The story of the beard-cloak, which Arthur wins in combat, is not repeated in Malory but is transformed into a slightly different tale.

In Malory, King Rience of Wales and Ireland has defeated eleven other kings and received their shaved beards in homage, which he used to 'purfle his mantle' (to trim his cloak – that is, to make a beard-fur collar for it). He has space for one more beard and demands that Arthur cut off his and send it to Rience as tribute, or else he will 'enter into his lands and burn and slay and never leave till he have his head and beard'. Arthur calls this 'the most villainous and lewdest message that ever man heard sent to a king' and warns that even though his beard is 'young yet to make a purfle of it', unless

Rience does homage to *him*, Arthur will have his head.

Beard-taking is clearly a form of substitute head-taking and an act of humiliation, but it is strange to see it back-projected into Arthurian times. In those days, the Romans were clean-shaven and the Gauls and Britons were said only to sport moustaches (at least by Caesar). There is a further curious incident involving hair in Malory's *Le Morte D'Arthur*. At one point in Lancelot's quest for the Holy Grail, he is advised to take the hair of a deceased holy man and place it next to his skin to provide supernatural protection. This he does, and is duly protected in his next encounter with villainy.

The final mystical act in Geoffrey is the dying Arthur's retreat to Avalon, which certainly casts doubt over Arthur's fate. Once again this incident is ripe for elaboration by subsequent writers who lavish it with the return of Excalibur to the lake, the arrival of the royal barge and Arthur's disappearance into the mists of time.

Geoffrey's work essentially generated two skeletons – the pseudo-historical and the purely mythical – which later writers embellished at their will. To the pseudo-historical they added a great array of characters – mostly knights of the round table, from Lancelot to Galahad, but also the mystic women like Arthur's sister Morgan Le Fay. To the purely mythical they embroidered a profusion of incidents and themes to flesh out the metaphysics. The Lady of the Lake, unseen in Geoffrey, is probably an accretion of the Celtic fertility goddess Nerthus, who receives sacrificial offerings of weapons and sometimes even humans in her sacred waters. It is strange, though, that both the sword in the stone motif and the Lady of the Lake giving and retrieving the votive sword, originate in the later versions of the legends, not in the Welsh-based tales of Geoffrey.

The quest for the Holy Grail, again unmentioned in Geoffrey, takes up more and more time and space in the later romances. Although it is given a strictly Christian veneer, the notion of a quest for a cup or chalice, attributed with healing and regenerative powers, has powerful pagan manifestations in many cultures of that period. But there are also many less well-known mystical motifs and incidents in the canon which cannot easily be traced to British Celtic folklore.

Many of these are found grouped together into a scenario which appears repeatedly in several variant forms. In essence there is a sacred site, usually a spring or fountain, usually within a grove of trees, though it may also be a ford, a crossroads, a bridge or a gateway. This lush 'Holy Grove' is contrasted with the wasteland and 'desert' surrounding it. It is the home of a fair and holy lady or damsel, who is often associated with the moon, the colour white and water – all symbols of purity. She is a semi-divine being.

On the site there may well be a 'pavilion' or circular tent with a conical roof. The tent is portrayed as a place of refuge. Guarding the woman and the Holy Grove is a fierce champion who will challenge any male who sets foot there. The woman's role in this challenge is ambiguous. She may see herself as a prisoner of her champion and may provoke the newcomer to combat. If the newcomer is victorious she may give herself up to him in her tent/pavilion, but she may also demand the head of her old champion which she takes and attaches to her saddle. The blood from this man, who has essentially sacrificed himself defending his divine woman, is said to have the power to heal.

This incident happens to Arthur in *Perlesvaus*, where Arthur is sent on a quest to a dangerous place by Guinevere. He comes to a gate leading to a beautiful clearing with a huge tree at its centre, where a fair damsel sits. She directs him to the chapel he seeks, but warns him that he will be challenged. A mounted black knight suddenly appears and hurls a fiery lance into Arthur's arm. Arthur's blood extinguishes the flames and he succeeds in killing the black knight.

Twenty knights then appear from the forest and hack the black knight's body to pieces. The damsel asks Arthur to fetch the head for her, which he does. She anoints Arthur's wound with the blood from the head, effecting an immediate cure. She then explains that she will be able to use the healing head to retrieve a castle which has been stolen from her by treachery, and departs carrying the head. In a later episode in *Perlesvaus*, a damsel travelling in a cart drawn by stags brings no less than 152 severed heads to king Arthur's court.

Some experts see in this series of events the chimes of very ancient pagan religious practices whereby strong men do battle to attain possession of a female deity. In their defeat they become sacrificial victims in honour of the goddess. This rather Darwinian clash of the fittest for sexual rights over the alpha female is also seen as lying at the roots of the notions of courtly love. It is certainly a theme played out constantly by the key figures in Arthur's tales.

Associated with this scenario is a much more widespread (and longer lasting) notion which links the fitness and virility of the king to the fitness and fertility of his nation. As his potency fails there is a need to replace him, by violence if necessary. The king is the microcosm of the state, the health of the two inextricably entwined. This is of course a timeless theme – Shakespeare's dramas are riddled with it, from *King Lear* to *Richard II*, and a host more of his histories and tragedies. It is also a recurrent obsession of our contemporary Press, which takes such delight in dissecting the personal, moral and sexual lives of the heirs to the British throne, implicitly linking them to the moral debasement of the nation.

Tents as female places of shelter and pleasure are important in these incidents, and in *Perlesvaus* there is even a 'Queen of the Tents'. She has a conversation with a Damsel of the Carts, and it seems that there is a strong association between women, tents and carts. The Damsel of the Carts is a vital figure in some of the tales, as she acts as the bearer of the Holy Grail. When she brings her cartload of severed heads to Arthur, it is – as mentioned above – drawn by stags. This association of women with stags also occurs in classical mythology where Diana, goddess of the chase, parades in a cart drawn by stags. The stag or hart (sometimes white and therefore even more mystical) is an important symbol of noble prey in many parts of the legends, and the animal is often associated with magic. In one of the tales Merlin covers himself in hair and temporarily becomes a stag.

Women are also associated with snakes or serpents. In one story a snake is transformed into a beautiful damsel, and Guinevere is likened to a crowned serpent, religious symbol of the 'Sarrassins', the ancient inhabitants of Britain before the coming of Arthur.

Besides their mystical links with snakes, severed heads, tents, carts and deer, these semi-divine damsels constantly advise, warn and guide the male combatants. Some of them, like the Lady of the Lake, bring up famous warriors, train them in martial skills and provide them with weapons. Lancelot, Galahad and Percival are all brought up and trained by supernatural females, and both Lancelot and Arthur receive their swords from females.

Once trained and armed, it is of course the main role of these young warriors to sally forth in quest of adventures, trials and heroic conflict. As already mentioned, this most frequently involves challenges to other knights who are typically guardians or captors of beguiling damsels, or are blocking the way forward at crossroads or fords.

The more dramatic encounters, however, involve conflict with supernatural beings such as giants, dragons and the like. The aims and goals of these adventures are frequently obscure, but where they are declared they are often to do with rescuing hostages and prisoners or seeking treasure. Above all, though, they are concerned with the adventure *per se* and with the tales that the knights will be able to tell once they return to Arthur's court. No matter what the context, Arthur invariably demands an account of all comers or returners to his court.

In these quests the combatants' weapons can take on supernatural qualities such as invincibility and unbreakability. They also frequently heat up, even becoming fiery, as in the case of the Black Knight who wounds Arthur with his fiery lance. In other instances, swords are associated with lightning bolts, and in this sense there is a certain equivalence between magic swords and celestial dragons, both capable of wreaking fiery havoc. Fiery weapons are also sometimes associated with castration.

By far the most elaborate and mystical of the knightly quests is of course the Grail Quest, or, as Malory calls it, the Sangrail – the 'blood-chalice' – Quest. In the French *Vulgate Cycle*, Joseph of Arimathea, the man who is said to have brought the Holy Grail to Britain, is wounded in the thighs by an angel with a countenance as bright as lightning. This story is repeated in many variants where kings who are guardians of the Grail are maimed by fiery weapons.

In a later episode in the *Vulgate*, the Grail is brought to Wales by Joseph of Arimathea's nephew, Alain le Gros, who is looking for empty land to settle on. Here he finds a land occupied only by small people who know nothing except how to cultivate the land. They are ruled over by a leprous king, who is cured by Alain and the Grail. In gratitude the king builds a castle for the Grail people and offers his daughter's hand to Alain's brother, Josué. They are married that same day and crowned king and queen of this 'Terre Foraine'. They receive the homage of the people, and that night they conceive a son and heir. On the same night the old king comes too close to the Holy Grail, provoking a man all covered in flames to hurl a lance at him which strikes him between the thighs, implicitly castrating him. In this way the succession passes safely into the hands of the new dynasty, and the fertility of the land is restored by the demise of the old infertile king resulting from the actions of the Grail itself.

Fire plays a part in another key incident in the Grail tales, when Galahad manages to extinguish a fire which burns continually in a tomb. That Galahad can extinguish this immortal flame signals to all that he must be the knight who will accomplish the Grail.

It has long been recognized that the Grail Quest is deeply connected to fertility cults associated with chalices and cauldrons, and that blood is seen to play a vital role in healing, regeneration and rejuvenation. It is also clear from the Grail Quest, and incidents such as Arthur's duel with the Black Knight, that women play an important part in this bloody healing process. Less frequently commented upon is the fact that the Grail is repeatedly associated with a specific name, or set of names. Alain le Gros is the first of many Alans, Alains, Elaines and the like to be associated with the Grail. As Joseph's nephew, he is the Grail's first guardian in Britain. He is also associated with a special lake where he ceremonially catches a fish, thus earning himself the title Rich Fisher, or the Fisher King. Alain le Gros in fact dies at the same time as the leper king, passing his role and title to his brother Josué.

Other male Alain manifestations are Helain the White, a Grail hero and Elian, prince of Ireland, who takes Lancelot's place at the round table after he elopes with Guinevere. Female Elaines also abound in extremely important places: the Lady of the Lake, who reared Lancelot, is called Elaine; Galahad's mother, who tricks Lancelot into impregnating her, is the Grail Bearer, named Elaine too. She appears in *Perlesvaus* as the Damsel of the Cart. Pellinor finds his daughter Eleine's severed head by a spring and takes it to Arthur's court. The fair maid who dies for love of Lancelot in the last section of the *Vulgate Cycle* – a central tragic figure later immortal-ized by Tennyson as The Lady of Shalott – is another Elaine. Helaine is the wife of king Ban and Lancelot's mother. Several other Elaine figures also appear in the tales, especially in association with Grail-challenged knights, although there are no clues in the stories as to why this should be.

By digging around in the darker, less well-known corners of the Arthurian legends I seem to have unearthed a series of elements – mentioned in the text above and summarized below – which do not add up simply as a reflection of early Celto-British beliefs, or as an admixture of those with Christian and classical Roman elements.

What I have found is certainly pagan, but not necessarily Celtic. A convenient explanation for this anomaly would be to consign all this stuff about Fisher-King Alans, who get their privates burnt off while swigging blood from magic chalices supplied by sumptuous damsels, to the realms of medieval fantasy. But that is *not* how I read it. To me, the way these themes appear, recur, get transformed from one story-teller to another, has the ring of mythology about it, not fantasy.

Mythology is about the representation of truths which lie beneath and beyond ordinary facts – deeper truths which people consider important enough to remember, conserve and pass on in narrative form. Arthur's stories, the most famous folk-tales in the world – still with us today, provoking people to think and write about them – are just that. They carry messages. And these messages have come from somewhere, but not perhaps from the obvious places. Although taken individually they seem fragmentary, when considered as a whole they provide us with the building blocks for constructing a rather elaborate culture with a specific way of looking at the world, all woven from the ideas we find on the pages of the Romances.

The defining element of this Arthurian society, then, is that it is horse-based. Chivalry, its guiding moral code, even carries the name 'horse'. The dominant characters are all warriors who are extremely mobile. Their most prized skills are martial – mounted feats of arms being the path to heroism and glory. Their most prized weapons are long, slashing, sometimes magical swords. The quest for virtue leads individuals and groups of men to undertake adventures which involve acts of ritual and real combat, both individually and as parts of a fighting force. Motivation for these quests is often stimulated by women, and typically involves the rescue of hostages or prisoners and the pursuit of wealth and treasures. Victory in battle is rewarded with the gift of lands where the recipient becomes the overlord of the local, farming-based peasantry (used as infantry during wars).

The world through which our heroes move is comprised of deserts and wastelands, with 'oases' of tree-clad groves with water sources. These islands of fecundity are the realms of women, many of them supernatural, living in tents or carts. And they are the places where blood is shed, heads taken and beards scalped in combat. Blood has the power to heal and regenerate, while the chalice – which holds it – has the power to maim, burn, castrate or kill. It is a world of fiery dragons, lightning and magical swords, a domain where men wield the weapons, while women – who may be pure, white and watery, but also snake-like demons who lust after human blood and heads – wield supernatural powers.

It is a dark world, but a fairly precisely painted one which derives some of its inspiration from the ancient Celts, but not all. It clearly has little or nothing to do with the world of Imperial Rome, although there are a few chimes at mythic levels with the ancient classical worlds. But we know that there was also another, quite distinct culture thriving on the eastern borders of the Roman Empire, a culture dismissed at the time as barbarian, until they first infiltrated, then thrust themselves upon western Europe.

I have noted that these people first made it to England quite early – about AD 170 – that their commander was called Artorius, and that they were heavy cavalrymen. There were a lot of them, around 5500 posted to guard Hadrian's Wall and Britain's northern defences. We know they carried the dragon as their standard and that in the fourth century AD the Romans adopted the barbarian title, *draconarius*, for their own cavalry, a title which still lingers in the British army in the form of 'dragoon'.

We know that after they had done their military service they stayed on in Britain, settling down especially at the veterans' fort which is now called Ribchester in Lancashire. With their horse-based culture and special connections to dragons and Arthur, these people look like they might just fit the bill. But the really important questions concern what was going on in their heads. Were they just barbarians, as the Romans certainly claimed, or were they much more 'civilized' than has previously been granted?

They were not literate, so we have the usual problems of interpreting second-hand reports about them and making inspired guesses about their ideology and aspirations. But these steppe nomads differ from the Celto-British contenders for Arthur's pedigree in one vital way. They have a rich and well-documented heritage – a complex and fascinating place in the development of the 'civilizations' of the Old World and a quite well-known history stretching back for 1500 years before Arthur reigned. To find out who they *really* were, we have to take a giant step back in time to around 800 BC – to the days when people were just beginning to ride horses . . .

CHAPTER FIVE

The Horse-Warriors

HORSEMANSHIP WAS SUCH AN INTEGRAL PART OF ARTHUR'S WORLD THAT it lent its name – chivalry – to its ideological core. Yet the peoples of Arthur's times who had the deepest and most intimate relations with horses were neither Celts nor Romans. They were, instead, the descendants of the first horse-riders.

Nobody knows exactly where and when people started riding horses, but, around 1000 BC, mounted cultures suddenly proliferated, giving the riders vastly increased freedom of movement. People were suddenly able to cover huge distances rapidly and with ease. The option to roam nomadically became real on a scale never experienced before. This single discovery transformed the societies of the horse-riders so radically that a new form of culture emerged. It is intriguing that this process of rapid cultural transformation repeated itself almost identically some 2500 years later, when the Spanish introduced horses to both North and South America. Within as little as a century, Native North and South Americans, on the plains in the North and the Pampas in the South, developed a totally new, highly mobile way of life.

That these were *new* developments goes rather against the grain of many people's assumptions about human social evolution. We tend to believe that our species started out as nomadic hunter-gatherers who then learnt to tame animals and wander with them, as nomadic herders. Only later did agriculture allow people to quit nomadism and settle down in fixed abodes. This sedentary way of life is seen as *the* essential prerequisite for the development first of village life then urban society, then urban-based 'ancient civilizations', and ultimately the modern world – us. This is certainly how the Romans saw it, how the 'civilizations' of the ancient Old World, both in the East and the West saw it. It is demonstrably not true.

Although debates continue about 'who did what when?', we know for sure that subsistence by hunting and gathering in the Old World was gradually transformed by the domestication of food plants. At the same time, around 10–12,000 years ago, people started to domesticate dogs. Some time later, around 8000 BC, sheep and goats entered the fold. A thousand years later, people tamed cattle. It is much less clear when we came into relatively friendly contact with the horse, nor exactly how this relationship evolved. The earliest tamings may have been around 4000 BC, and the current thinking is that people probably first used horses as pack and draught animals, as well as sources of meat, milk, leather and the like.

It is absolutely clear, however, that throughout this long period of acquiring and restraining plants and animals, people were living relatively sedentary lives, tending their fields and animals from fixed village bases. They were not, and could not be, highly nomadic. The first signs of using oxen as draught animals to pull ploughs appear around 4500 BC, and about 1000 years later the first ox-drawn carts and wagons appear. The arrival of animal-drawn transport made the possibility of moving home easier, and carts and wagons were enthusiastically adopted by one emergent language-group, the Indo-Europeans. Both the steppe nomads and the Celtic Britons spoke Indo-European languages.

From a disputed starting point either in the Near East or on the steppes, people speaking Indo-European languages were gradually fanning out from about 4000 BC, occupying western and central Asia as far as north India and the Chinese borders, as well as penetrating both the Mediterranean basin and north-west Europe. But this was not happening at speed. The Indo-European Diaspora took place over centuries and millennia, not weeks, months or years. Even the development of the fast, lightweight chariot, around 2000 BC, did not trigger a sudden upsurge in human mobility, probably because they are unstable vehicles.

But when people mastered the art of *riding* horses then things really began to change fast. A man or a woman riding a horse – and leading one or two changes of mount – could comfortably cover fifty kilometres in a day, and continue at this pace almost indefinitely. So in a month a rider could cover nearly 1500 kilometres; in two months he or she could ride from the Black Sea to Siberia. More importantly, the greater 'range' that horse-riding provided meant that people could exploit territory which had previously been inaccessible. They could cross dry areas, such as deserts, from water-source to water-source and ascend high up to mountain pastures which pedestrian herders could not reach. They and their herds could enter and leave terrain which was seasonally hostile – too hot, too cold, too dry – and use it during clement seasons only, retreating to milder climate zones at the height of summer or winter.

They also soon discovered that they could use their new-found mobility to great advantage when conflicts arose. Notions like 'attack' and 'retreat' take on an entirely new complexion from the back of a horse. So once people could ride horses, the nomadic way of life, abandoned by our hunter-gatherer forebears millennia before, once again offered obvious advantages to those who chose that path. There was nothing 'backward', 'primitive' or 'barbarian' about this move to nomadic pastoralism. It was a social step forwards, an 'evolution' to a new form of society and culture.

The most likely place where this revolution took place was on the steppes of western and central Asia. Here there were abundant herds of hardy wild horses which people had been hunting at least since the end of the Ice Age. And here too was abundant grazing land which could not be reached until people learnt how to ride. So the people of the steppes had plenty to gain by increasing their mobility.

As yet, though, we have only a hazy archaeological record to show us exactly when and where people began riding horses, revolving around the presence of pieces of horse harness etc., in graves and in the occasional discovery of horses' teeth worn by rubbing against a bit. There are problems with this latter evidence, as artistic representations show horses wearing bits pulling chariots from at least 1300 BC, so the presence of bits or bit-wear is not in itself evidence of people *riding* horses. However, this is not an unsurpassable problem, as horse-riding places different stresses on the bone and muscular structure of both horse and rider. Future careful examinations of skeletal remains should help to pinpoint the date of the first horse-riders.

By the time these early riders were appearing another development had occurred which is crucial for the unravelling of our story of Arthur: in many parts of the world people had learnt to write, and they were beginning to record events as they unfolded. The horse people of the steppes were not literate, but many of their neighbours to the east, south and west were.

We first hear about them in written sources from the Assyrians and Medes, living in city states of what is now Iran and Iraq. They talk of a people they call the Cimmerians – mounted nomads who spoke a language from the Iranian branch of the Indo-European language family. The Cimmerians were first reported living on the steppes to the north of the Caucasus, their territory extending as far west as the northern shores of the Black Sea. Yet even in these very early days, perhaps as early as 1300 BC, the Cimmerians were not alone. They were apparently being pushed off the steppes by a more powerful group of mounted warriors, the Scythians. The latter were in turn under pressure from a third powerful mounted people, the Massagetae, all of them apparently on the move to the west or south.

What was going on? Was there some unseen pump pushing these people westward or were they drawn by the magnet of the rich lands and cultures of the Near East and Europe?

The answer to these questions is complex. On the one hand the conversion to nomadic pastoralism was certainly successful. Experts have calculated that herder groups were able to expand their ranges at least five-fold with the coming of horse-riding. Herd sizes increased and surpluses of meat, dairy products, wool, leather and live animals became available for trade and barter.

Secondly, nomadic lifestyles have always tended to be healthier than sedentary farming, because people do not have to deal with the problems of waste disposal. Early farming communities suffered from disease simply because they lived amid their own disease-inducing detritus. Nomads leave it behind when they move on; and also tend to move away – disperse – when they hear of the arrival of epidemic diseases. Sedentary farmers cannot do this. So general health and survival rates among nomadic children would have been high and the population would therefore have increased. This meant that to survive, these peoples had to expand their territories, either by utilizing previously unused lands or by pushing out those who stood before them.

On the other hand, pastoral nomads are entirely dependent on the continual supply of two natural elements: pasture and water. While some food crops can survive for weeks without rain, animals cannot survive beyond a few days without water. From the ninth century BC onwards, the climate on the steppes was getting cooler and drier. So the nomads were probably moving westwards in search of better pastures and adequate water as the drier areas of central Asia became colder, more arid and less hospitable to the horse nomads and their herds. When the climate turned warmer and wetter in the fifth century BC, this allowed the nomads to expand on to the (previously arid) south Russian steppes.

A third factor was not so much the 'push' of population growth and climatic change as the 'pull' of the cultures which lay at the edges of the nomads' territories. If you were travelling, as these nomads did, westwards from perhaps as far east as southern Siberia, there would have been little to distract you on the vast plains of central Asia. But if (as they did) you were to turn south at the western edge of the Caspian Sea and skirt down the eastern edge of the Caucasian mountains, then you would suddenly find yourself in Persia, lands in those days of the Medes, Assyrians and Babylonians – powerful warlike city-states with urban-based, literate cultures, splendid buildings, works of art and treasures. If you were to press on through these lands (as some of the nomads eventually did) you would come to Syria, Palestine and the frontiers of the most complex, sophisticated civilization in the world, the Empire of the Pharaohs of Egypt.

A few hundred years later, if instead of turning south through the narrow passes of the Caucasus, you simply carried on westward you would come to the new colonies which the Greeks were setting up around the shores of the Black Sea. In fact, when the Greeks first penetrated these lands, the horse-warriors were already in possession of them. Once the Greeks had set up shop, the nomads were immediately drawn to their fine handicrafts and took a great shine to their wine. So the lure of the jewellery, metalwork, pottery, wine, oil and spices of the classical world pulled the nomads west and south, just as, 3000 miles away, the lure of silk and other luxury goods drew their cousins eastward into China.

These, then, seem to be the elements which set the stage when the curtain of prehistory is first drawn back on the nomads from the east, around 700 BC. This was probably only a few centuries after these people had mastered the art of horse-riding, but they were already at ease in the saddle.

The earliest records we have of the nomads are Assyrian, who recorded contact with first the Cimmerians then later with the Scythians in the eighth century BC. Homer also mentions them in the *Odyssey*, probably referring to the ninth century BC. It seems that several attempted incursions into Assyrian territory were repulsed, but after a defeat in about 670 BC a large body of Cimmerian cavalry were subsequently recruited as mercenaries by the Assyrians, and took part in many successful conquests in the Near East over the following fifty years. Sometimes acting independently under their own king, sometimes in alliance with more powerful local leaders, and sometimes as vassals of the latter, the Cimmerians were experimenting with a series of different forms of

politico-military alliance, a pattern of behaviour which their successors continued and elaborated.

Although the Assyrians left us the skeleton of their political
manoeuvres, comparatively little is known about these peoples from
contemporary sources. But two centuries later the great Greek
historian Herodotus decided to track down the origins of the
ongoing conflict between the Greeks and the Persians. Fortunately
Herodotus was not only a great historian and detective, he was also
an excellent observer of contemporary life and excelled in the art of
ethnography. Sensing the importance of the role of the eastern
nomads in shaping the history of this period, he not only traced
their origins, but also travelled north to the Black Sea to meet the
living Scythian nomads, to get the story 'from the horse's mouth' as
it were. His detailed records are absolutely pivotal in our understanding of these people, and without them it would be impossible to
trace any relationship between these early nomads and the Arthurian
epic.

At the beginning of Herodotus's first book, he pinpoints the root
of the tension between Greece and Persia as being the Greek refusal
to recognize that 'the Persians claim Asia and the barbarian races
dwelling in it as their own. Europe and the Greek states being, in
their opinion, quite separate and distinct from them.'

A few paragraphs later, Herodotus records the Cimmerian
intrusion into Assyria and their defeat and eventual expulsion.
Later, he mentions that the Cimmerians were not a single people,
but divided in two, between the 'kings and royals' and the
'Cimmerian people' (commoners). He tells us that when threatened by the Scythians the 'kings and royals', repulsed by the
prospect of being turned into slaves, decided to defend their lands
to the last man, but the 'common people' decided to make a run
for it south into Persia. Having annihilated the 'royal' Cimmerians

the Scythians then set off in pursuit of the 'commoners'.

This division of the Cimmerians into royals and commoners has prompted some experts to think that the two groups were originally two distinctive peoples, the royals having imposed themselves upon the 'commoners' some time before. This suggests that even from the earliest times nomad society was hierarchical. The form it takes is also instructive, as this propensity to overcome then dominate subject peoples is a recurrent characteristic of all the subsequent horse-nomad societies, right up until the times of the supposed Arthur.

According to Herodotus, the Scythians took the wrong route south in their pursuit of the commoner Cimmerians – taking the mountain road while their quarries hugged the coast (of the Caspian Sea). Arriving in Media, the Scythians did battle with the Medes and defeated them: 'they (the Medes) lost their power in Asia, which was taken over in its entirety by the Scythians'.

Herodotus then ascertains that the Scythian rule of 'Asia' (the Near East) lasted for the following twenty-eight years. During this time, they roamed as far as the frontiers of the Egyptian Empire in Palestine where the Pharaoh Psammeticus met them. By a combination of earnest entreaties and bribery he persuaded them to come no further, and they turned to sacking Syria instead. There, a small detachment of the raiders took a detour and sacked the most holy temple of Aphrodite Urania. In revenge the goddess inflicted them with:

what is called the 'female disease' and their descendants still suffer from it. This is the reason the Scythians give for this mysterious complaint, and travellers to the country can see what it is like. The Scythians call those who suffer from it 'Enarees'.

These 'Enarees' were evidently men who had been rendered impotent, possibly by spending too long in the saddle and wearing too tight-fitting trousers. Many of them were transvestites and the Scythians respected them as prophets and seers. Impotent men do of course play a part in the Arthurian legends, although they are mostly castrated kings who have renounced their power to the ascendant following generation. We should note, though, that in both cases these are men who have surrendered their martial powers.

According to Herodotus, the Scythians continued to raise hell throughout the region and he says that their twenty-eight-year reign of:

> violence and neglect of the law led to absolute chaos. Apart
> from tribute arbitrarily imposed and forcibly extracted they
> behaved like mere robbers, riding up and down the country and
> seizing people's property.

In the end, the Median king invited them to a banquet, got the Scythians drunk, then murdered them to regain power over his country. It is curious – but probably coincidental – that this is exactly how the Saxon Hengist tricked and slaughtered hundreds of British nobles at a 'peace conference' on Salisbury Plain just before Merlin's appearance in Geoffrey of Monmouth's *The History of the Kings of Britain*.

Evidently, however, some of the Scythians did escape as Herodotus picks up their story in book four of his histories. Here he tells us that the Scythian women, left behind on the steppes when their men went to raid Persia, had become bored – not surprisingly, as the menfolk were away for twenty-eight years. So the women decided to marry and procreate with their slaves. The half-slave children, hearing of the return of the menfolk from Persia, resolved to try to resist them. They dug and manned a defensive ditch across the northern pass out of the Caucasian mountains. The Scythian men, coming upon it, at first decided to attack, but then reasoned that this would cause unnecessary loss of life to both themselves and their slaves. So instead they rode forward unarmed but cracking their whips loudly and threateningly. This immediately made the slaves remember their station in life, and they ran away, abandoning their defences. So the Scythians were reunited with their womenfolk and order, of their sort, was restored.

Although this is the way Herodotus tells it, we do not know for sure that only Scythian men went on this twenty-eight-year raid, nor do we know precisely who the Scythian 'slaves' who stayed behind were. It is, however, quite possible that they were farming people previously subjugated by the Scythians. The fact that their sons chose to build and man a defensive ditch (an infantry tactic), rather than meet the returning warriors on horseback, also suggests that this section of Scythian society was not mounted. Other reports elsewhere confirm that the Scythians did sometimes put infantry into battle, men who presumably travelled by cart, and who were also clearly seen as inferior to their mounted 'masters'.

Close scrutiny of Assyrian records reveals a much more convoluted (and precise) tale than the history reported by Herodotus. According to these, in the early seventh century BC, a coalition of Mannaeans, Cimmerians and Medes had formed against Assyria but the Assyrian king wooed the Scythians into an alliance. By 652, the latter two had defeated their enemies and subjugated them. The alliance had been cemented by the marriage of the Assyrian king's daughter to the Scythian king Bartatua. Once the Medes had been beaten, the Assyrian king gave their country to the Scythians to rule.

By 645 BC, the Scythians were at the height of their power in

'Asia', married into the royal family and unquestionably experiencing strong cultural influences from this rich and complex society – influences they would carry back to the steppes and beyond some fifty years later. It was during this period that the Scythians adopted the practice of carrying a short sword, called an *Akinake*, while mounted and also started to use the three-sided bronze arrow heads which were to become their 'trademark' all over western Asia. The magnificent stone Assyrian bas-reliefs in the British Museum clearly depict Scythian warriors firing their arrows from galloping horses. Several of them have turned round and are firing backwards, a feat so extraordinary that it too is a hallmark of their renowned equestrian martial skills.

In 1947, Persian archaeologists excavated a strongly fortified castle and found at its centre a large bronze coffin bearing images which almost certainly represent the Scythian king Bartatua. He had of course derived his status and wealth from the Assyrians, but as their power waned – in about 620 BC – the Scythians defected and joined forces with their old subjects, the Medes. This tipped the balance of power in the latter's favour and led directly to the downfall of the Assyrians. The Medes then turned on their erstwhile allies, finally managing to drive the Scythians out around 590 BC.

Even though the archaeological data and extant documents are pretty thin on the ground, we can already start to piece together a picture of the Scythians which has some clear echoes with the 'theoretical' Arthurian society I outlined at the end of Chapter Four. This is a fully fledged highly nomadic warrior society which relies almost entirely for its success on horses. It has already developed its mounted martial skills to the point where it will take on the disciplined and organized (though mainly infantry) forces of large-scale urban societies and, as often as not, win.

All depictions strongly suggest that individuals fight while mounted, and do not just use their mounts to get to and around the field. Their hierarchical social order is dominated by an aristocratic, mounted warrior caste. These warriors have developed their own extremely mobile military tactics, centring around lightning strikes followed by rapid retreats if needs be – hence the Scythian horse-archers firing backwards in the Assyrian carved reliefs.

At this stage in time, they are most famed as archers, but have adopted the habit of wearing swords suspended from straps attached to their belts. Other than the spoils of pillaging we can assume that subsistence is based on herding, and that this activity is carried out by either women or slaves or both. Given that the men feel free to go off raiding for at least twenty-eight years, we can safely assume a good deal of autonomy for their womenfolk. It follows that they too would be skilled riders and probably capable of mounting their own defence.

Their leaders have discovered the relative ease with which they can raid and pillage, but have also found that their élite (but numerically limited) cavalry can hold the balance of power when roughly even forces from urban nation-states face each other. The cavalry is all too often the decisive factor. The rewards for being on the winning side are disproportionately good. With the apportioning of entire subject nations to their control, they have discovered the most rapid and effective means of achieving wealth and power. They have learnt a good deal too about how a small but feared minority can dominate a large but subservient majority.

Another point of considerable interest is that at the height of their power in 'Asia', when the Scythians were presumably more sedentary, they had clearly experimented with using a very heavily fortified base – a castle from which to sally forth to raise tribute or raid and plunder. The echoes with Arthurian times are here both surprising and revealing. All these factors have led experts to conclude that by the sixth century BC the Scythians were one of the most militarily and politically powerful peoples in the world.

The notion of forming war-bands to go off on adventures, questing for treasure and enhanced social status, *the* most prevalent Arthurian preoccupation, was well established in this culture. The desire to learn about exotic fantastical places and beings may have also contributed to their wanderlust. In the Arthurian quests, Arthur and his knights frequently came across extraordinarily exotic lands populated by many types of weird mythical beasts. This would certainly have been the experience of the Scythian questers as they rode into the heart of ancient Persia. The surviving doors and wall plaques of the Assyrian temples and palaces attest to an extremely elaborate metaphysical cosmology bristling with exotic beasts – eagle-men, sphinxes, griffins and many more magical beasts abound alongside the more prosaic elegies to the military victories of their kings.

The Assyrian magical bestiary comprised many creatures which were essentially composite – heads of one animal combined with the body of another, talons of a third and so on. Although it is probable that the Scythians had already developed their own artistic tradition, known as the 'animal style', by the time they pushed south into 'Asia', there is little evidence of them taking their indigenous style southwards with them. But when they left, they carried in their heads and their saddle-bags looted images and tales of mythical beasts which would haunt their people for generations to come, and would, in my view, play a major part in both the Arthurian legends and in the formation of the mystical medieval code of heraldry.

Perhaps more important than the images themselves, the Scythians had been subjected to forms of magical thinking among the Assyrians which may well have altered their view of the greater world – the world of the divinities. We do not know enough about them to be sure of how they thought when they arrived in Persia, but we do know – and can see for ourselves – what they saw there. No one can stroll past those magical works of art without appreciating another totally supernatural world unfolding before their eyes. We know, too, that these images did indeed impress themselves upon the Scythians, as composite beasts start to appear in their works of art and decoration directly after their return to the steppes from Persia.

The next mention Herodotus makes of the nomads dates to about 530 BC, seventy or so years after the Scythians left Persia. By this time the Persian king Cyrus is determined to subjugate the Massagetae, the nomads who had forced the Scythians westwards more than a century earlier. As is Herodotus's wont, he mixes in anecdotal information about these people as he unfolds this particular piece of history. He first explains that they are numerous and warlike, a part of the Scythian nation living beyond the river Araxes (Oxus) on the eastern side of the Caspian Sea. He then immediately highlights a special discovery they have made – a tree:

Whose fruit has a very odd property: for when they have parties and sit round the fire, they throw some of it into the flames, and as it burns it smokes like incense, and the smell of it makes them drunk just as wine does the Greeks; and they get more and more intoxicated as more fruit is thrown on until they jump up and start dancing and singing. Such, at least are the reports on how these people live.

In short, the Massagetae were dope-smokers. Wild cannabis grows in many parts of central Asia and there is plenty more evidence for the nomads' use of the plant. While there is no evidence that this particular cultural trait made its way into the Arthurian canon, the ritual use of intoxicants generally seems to lead to a heightened awareness of the possibility of other, non-ordinary planes of consciousness and experience – planes where dragons may indeed dwell and human blood cures people.

Returning to the story, Herodotus tells us that when Cyrus first decided to subjugate the Massagetae they were ruled by a queen, Tomyris, who had succeeded her husband. Cyrus's first ploy is to ask for her hand in marriage. She sees through the ruse and refuses him, then sends a message to him saying she knows his game. She warns him not to take her on, but says that if battle is inevitable then it should take place well within his or her territory, not on the banks of the frontier river, the Araxes. Cyrus's advisers counsel him to agree to this and lay a trap for the Massagetae. Once the Massagetae forces have withdrawn from the river-frontier, the Persians set up a huge banquet on tables then withdraw out of sight, leaving only a small guard by the feast. The plan is based on the nomads' ingenuousness, they having 'no experience of such luxuries as the Persians enjoy and know nothing about the pleasures of life'. The ruse works: about a third of the Massagetaen army wipes out the Persian guard and gets thoroughly bloated and intoxicated on the food and wine left as bait. The Persians then fall on them, slaughter a great number and take many prisoners, including queen Tomyris's son.

Hearing of this deceitful defeat, Tomyris pours scorn on Cyrus and demands that he return her son and leave her lands. 'If you refuse,' she adds, 'I swear by the sun our master to give you more blood than you can drink, for all your gluttony.' Cyrus ignores her threats but allows her son's hands to be untied. As soon as they are free of the bonds, he kills himself. When Tomyris hears of her son's death she summons the remaining two-thirds of her army and engages the Persians in pitch battle. After a fearsome struggle, the Massagetae carry the day and Cyrus is killed. Tomyris orders her troops to search the battlefield for Cyrus's body. Once it is found, the queen takes Cyrus's head and pushes it into a skin which had been filled with human blood, fulfilling her threat.

To conclude book one, Herodotus rounds off the story of the nomads' victory over the Persians with a few more anecdotes about their culture. He mentions that they employ both cavalry and infantry, although clearly the cavalry predominate. They know and work gold and bronze, both of which are plentiful in their lands, and they decorate their horses' breastplates, bridles and bits with gold. He also claims that, although they marry, they are promiscuous and if a man desires another man's wife all he need do is 'hang up his quiver in front of her wagon then enjoy her without misgivings'. Old men also choose when to die, each one gathering his relatives to a party where he is included . . . 'in the general sacrifice of cattle: then they boil the flesh and eat it. This they consider to be the best sort of death.' Finally he concludes that 'The only god they worship is the sun, to which they sacrifice horses: the idea behind this is to offer the swiftest of mortal creatures to the swiftest of the gods'.

So, in this episode, we have a reliable description of a full-blown defeat of a 'civilized' nation by 'barbarian' mounted nomads in the year 530 BC. More revealingly, we encounter a powerful woman demanding the head of a vanquished enemy and deliberately associating herself with human blood. In passing, we learn that women evidently enjoy a considerable degree of sexual and political autonomy; and their domain is clearly established as the wagon. Finally, we learn that men perform a sort of self-sacrifice when they are no longer able to contribute sexually or economically to their community.

Looking back to the Arthurian canon, every one of these motifs are to be found there. Queen Tomyris could almost have been the Damsel of the Cart, demanding and receiving the head of the vanquished enemy, and using human blood for mystical purposes – in this case revenge. The old men sacrifice themselves, just as many of the failed and vanquished knights and kings do in the Arthurian tales.

Herodotus's tales return to the Scythians in the year 512 BC, just about twenty years before his own birth. The Persian king Darius, having conquered the lands to the south and west of the Black Sea, reached the Danube and decided to press on into Scythia, apparently to avenge the Scythian twenty-eight-year raid on Media a century earlier. The Scythians, learning of Darius's plans, summoned all their nomadic neighbours and asked them to join in a single alliance to take on the huge army of the Persians. Some agreed to join the Scythians – the Geloni, Budini and Sauromatae, all of them people we might call semi-autonomous members of the steppe nomad confederation. Others, also members of this unstable coalition, considered the Scythians had brought the Persian trouble on themselves by raising hell down south in the first place, so they refused to join the alliance and returned home. These were the Agathyrsi, the Neuri, Androphagi ('flesh eaters'), Melanchlaeni and Tauri.

Realizing that they did not have the manpower to defeat the

Persians in open battle, the Scythians decided to lead them a merry dance. Sending their women and children in their mobile wagon-homes out in front, along with their herds, they allowed Darius to cross the Danube and drew him right towards the lands of the tribes who had refused to support their alliance, always staying a day's march in front of the Persians, blocking up all the wells and springs as they went.

This ruse worked well, forcing the uncommitted neighbouring tribes either to flee or to join the Scythian alliance until they reached the Agathyrsi, who fortified their frontier and told the Scythians if they entered their land they would be attacked and driven out. So the Scythians just melted away and headed off in a different direction. Eventually Darius became so tired and frustrated by running round after the Scythians that he sent their king, Idanthyrus, a letter accusing him of cowardice and challenging the Scythians to stand and fight or submit and become slaves. Idanthyrus's reply is the quintessence of the nomads' credo, perfectly highlighting the culture-clash between the two ways of life:

Persian, I have never run from any man in fear; and I am not doing so now from you. There is, for me, nothing unusual in what I have been doing: it is precisely the sort of life I always lead, even in times of peace. If you want to know why I won't fight you I will tell you: in our country there are no towns and no cultivated land; fear of losing which, or seeing it ravaged, might indeed provoke hasty battle . . . and as for your being my master I acknowledge no masters but Zeus from whom I sprang and Hestia the Scythian queen . . . your claim to being my master is easily answered – be damned to you!

The Scythians were so incensed by Darius's threat of slavery that they decided to start harassing the Persians every time they went out foraging. Herodotus notes that:

> on every occasion the Scythian cavalry proved superior to the Persian, which would give ground and fall back to the infantry for support; this checked the attack, for the Scythians knew the Persian infantry would be too much for them, and regularly turned tail after driving in the cavalry.

The ongoing harassment had the desired effect of running down both the supplies and the morale of the Persians, and things reached a head when the Scythians apparently drew up their army in full battle order, ready to fight. But as the Persians were taking up their positions a hare broke loose on the battlefield. The Scythians evidently enjoyed nothing better than mounted hare-coursing, and squadron after squadron shot off in pursuit of the small but agile creature. Soon the entire field was reduced to 'a shouting rabble'. Darius, after finding out what the fuss was all about, finally realized in what contempt the Scythians held him and decided that it was 'time to think of the best way of getting out of this country in safety'. His army retreated ignominiously, the Scythians harassing them all the way, and only narrowly averted a disaster when crossing the Danube out of Scythian territory.

In military terms, it is clear that the Scythians were master tacticians who had developed the art of mobile warfare to a state of near perfection. Some 200 years after Darius's failed campaign, the Chinese military strategist Sun Tsu, a man most professional soldiers recognize as the greatest military genius ever to have lived, would write the following in *The Art of War* :

An Assyrian king (right) pursues mounted steppe warriors, characteristically firing their bows backwards as their horses gallop away, from ninth century BC (British Museum)

Top of an Etruscan wine mixer, showing four prancing Scythian warriors, evidence that their fame had spread as far as Italy by the fifth century BC (British Museum)

Greek vase depicting a centaur with marked Scythian characteristics - his beard, the recurved bow and the hares he has shot (British Museum)

Golden griffin-dragon in the animal style. From the Oxus Treasure, fifth century BC (British Museum)

Gilded silver bowl depicting Scythian men in pairs relaxing together, fourth century BC (Novosti/London)

Reverse of the same bowl, an intimate scene showing a man bandaging, or perhaps putting leggings on, his friend (Novosti/London)

Scythian golden pectoral, magnificently worked with real and magical animals and scenes of daily life, fourth century BC (Novosti/London)

Paired griffins in animal style, also from the Oxus treasure (British Museum)

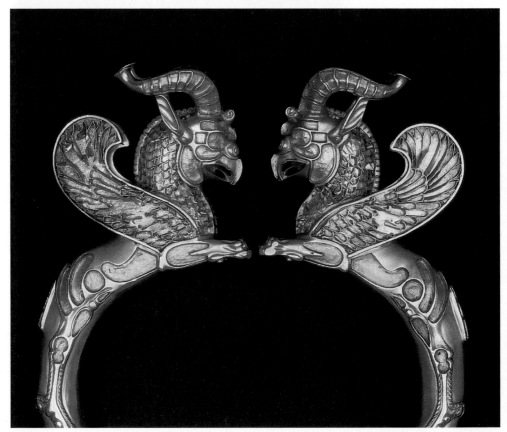

Detail from pectoral (left), showing men, with bows in cases, treating a fleece, domestic animals and griffins ravaging horses (Novosti/London)

Sarmatian princess's treasure necklace, depicting a bearded man with a long sword balanced across his lap. Eagle-headed warriors do battle with dragons on either side (Novosti/London)

Detail of the same necklace. The bodies of the eagle-people and the borders of the piece were originally decorated with inset gemstones (Novosti/London)

Sarmatian cavalryman wielding a typical dragon windsock battle standard, second century AD, found in northern England (Chester City Council)

Medieval portrait of King Arthur (British Library)

Scythian warrior, from the Oxus treasure (British Museum)

Fight between king Arthur and the Roman Emperor (British Library)

The bloody battle of Camlann, where Arthur killed Mordred and was himself mortally wounded (British Library)

'...and then he threw the sword as far into the water as he might; and there came an arm and an hand above the water and met it, and caught it, and so shook it thrice and brandished, and then vanished away the hand with the sword in the water' Sir Thomas Malory *Le Mort D'Arthur* (British Library)

To win one hundred victories in one hundred battles is not the acumen of skill. To subdue the enemy without fighting is the acumen of skill.

This was precisely what the outnumbered Scythians had done to Darius and his army.

This interlude in Herodotus's narrative also gives us a good sense of the relations between the Scythians and their neighbours. They were evidently one of many similar steppe nomad groups who broadly shared a common culture and probably spoke related languages of the Iranian branch of the Indo-European family. These were autonomous groups who were evidently capable of close co-operation and an integrated command structure once alliances had been formed. Alternatively they also reserved the right to remain outside any larger coalition if they so chose.

Herodotus tells us that one group had a large town made mostly of wood which the Persians burnt down. This is thought to be a site now known as Belsk, where a huge earthwork rampart enclosed a major city, so some of the steppe peoples were urbanized. However, Herodotus makes it abundantly clear that the leaders adhered to the ideology of the free-roaming nomad unencumbered by territory or property.

Overall, the patterns of political organization and inter-group relations of the steppe nomads are very similar to the relations between neighbouring kingdoms in the Arthurian tales, with highly mobile equestrian élites playing out the great games of political and military dice. Success depended upon making and maintaining alliances with autonomous neighbouring powers. Only when such a venture was successful did any one group feel that decisive military action could be taken.

It was almost certainly because of their shared hostility to the Persians that (the Greek) Herodotus repeatedly gives the Scythians, Massagetae and the other steppe nomads a good press. But he was also evidently genuinely intrigued by them, so much so that he actually travelled to the Black Sea to meet them and set aside almost the whole of book four of his *Histories* for a detailed ethnographic account of what he saw and heard.

Like all good enquirers of those times, the question of origins, of pedigree, is always to the forefront when establishing a people's place in the overall schema of things. The Greeks, having established mythological space-time as the immediate precursor of their own historical time, looked for and usually found the same phenomenon with other ethnic entities.

Surprisingly, Herodotus asserts that the Scythians claim to be the youngest of all nations and gives three versions of their origins. In the first, a son of Zeus and a daughter of the river Borysthenes were the first inhabitants of Scythia, which was empty before they arrived. They had three sons and during their reign four golden objects suddenly fell from the sky – a golden plough, a golden yolk, a golden battle axe and a golden cup. When the two older sons attempted to pick up these objects they burst into flames. When the youngest approached he was able to handle them, so he became recognized as the legitimate successor to the throne. From his line were descended the royal Scythians, the most powerful of the Scythian sub-groups in Herodotus's time. There were three other 'clans' descended from the older brothers, including the 'agricultural Scythians' who farmed grain on the northern fringes of the Black Sea.

Another account of Scythian origins relates that Heracles strayed into their territory one evening and turned loose his chariot-horses to graze while he slept. In the morning he could not find them, but as he searched he came to a place called 'The Woodland' where dwelt a snake-woman in a cave. She was human from the buttocks upwards, but a snake below the waist. She told him she had his horses and would return them to him if he first made love to her. This he did, and she kept him captive for as long as it took for her to conceive three sons by him. As he left, he ordered the snake-woman to test the three boys when they grew up, using Heracles's bow, girdle and buckle. The two older boys, Agathyrsi and Gelonus (two of the outsider clans listed when the Scythians called for them to resist the Persians) failed the test and were sent into exile, but the youngest, Scythes, succeeded and established the royal line which had persisted for 1000 years from its foundation until Darius's failed incursion into Scythia.

This motif of a serpent-queen and serpent-women occurs several times in the Arthurian canon, and in the *Vulgate* Guinevere is likened to a crowned serpent.

Finally, Herodotus offers a much more prosaic account of Scythian origins which he thinks is most likely the truth. He says they were pushed out of their homeland around the Sea of Azov by the Massagetae, so they invaded the land of the Cimmerians and forced them to flee into northern Media, setting in train the 'history' we have already traced. But the underlying engine for this process he sees essentially as the knock-on, domino effect of successive 'tribes' moving westwards, each one encroaching on the territory of the one in front.

Having established the historical dynamics of the situation, Herodotus then casts his eye around the immense geography of the region, listing the major 'tribal' and sub-tribal groups, the nature of the terrain and the lie of the land, its rivers and so forth. To give colour to the places and the peoples, he never tires of providing anecdotes about local customs. Some of these seem far-fetched – the Arimaspians are said to be one-eyed, and at the easternmost borders of the nomads' domains are said to be 'the Griffins which guard the Gold'. But in recent centuries experts have been repeatedly staggered to find that these assertions contain some grains of truth, so we need to take even Herodotus's more outlandish statements seriously.

One of the most recent cases, for example, concerns the 'Griffins which guard the Gold'. Until a few years ago, it was assumed that these beasts were entirely fictitious, although it was known that gold had been exported from Siberia since the days of Herodotus. So the location of the gold far to the east was right. Griffins are in essence eagle-headed, four-legged beasts with wings and claws as talons. The recent upsurge in interest in dinosaurs has revealed that the earliest form of bird-dinosaurs conform pretty much to the stereotype image of the griffin – four-legged beasts with huge beaks and skulls, long tails and wings. Furthermore, their skeletons can be found on the surface of the Gobi desert in considerable numbers, and they were presumably visible there 2000 years ago. So it may well be that Herodotus was right: that those who guarded the gold aimed to frighten away adventurers by telling of dinosaur-birds and may even have produced skeletons as 'proof'.

Herodotus himself takes care to distinguish between events he is fairly certain are accurate, either because he saw them himself or they were reported to him by first-hand witnesses, and those details which were mere hearsay and quite likely exaggerated or fabricated.

Before we take a closer look at the reported customs of the Scythians and their neighbours, we should briefly assess the state of play when Herodotus gathered this information, around 450 BC. By this time the Greeks had several well-established colonies on the north side of the Black Sea, in Scythian territory. There essentially as traders, relations between them and the Scythians were in general amicable.

The Greeks sought the abundant supplies of fish from the rivers and the large surpluses of grain which the agricultural Scythians produced. This grain supply was in fact essential for the sustenance of the Aegean Greek motherland. The Greeks also traded with the Scythians for their furs, gold and slaves. Slaves were clearly taken in warfare, but may also have been exacted as tribute from the many groups of agriculturalists who were dominated by the Scythians. These people farmed the more sheltered and better watered areas under the Scythians' control, mostly in the forest steppes to the north of the grasslands where the pastoralists prevailed.

Although relations between the Greeks and Scythians were cordial, it is abundantly clear that the Scythians were very proud of their own culture and traditions and were opposed to cultural convergence. Herodotus tells of one Scythian king who, developing a taste for Greek rituals on visits to their towns, began to stay for several days and to dress in the flowing loose clothes of the Greeks rather than the tight-fitting trousers, jerkins and capes of his own people. Some time later some of his people spied him so dressed and reported it to their fellow Scythians. As soon as the king returned to his people he was arraigned and killed. The Scythians were certainly proud of their separate ethnic identity.

None the less, they were also drawn to the superb craftsmanship of the Greek metal and ceramics workers, and many of their leaders were seriously rich. At the time Herodotus visited them, the Scythians were beginning to commission Greek craftsmen to produce decorated objects, many of gold, which, although made in Greek style, depicted scenes from the everyday lives of their Scythian patrons. Some of this gold work is of staggeringly fine artistic quality, and also provides us with a magnificent record of Scythian life.

Herodotus was aware that some acculturation was taking place between the Greeks and Scythians, and refers to two groups as Graeco-Scythians, but he makes no mention of the beautiful hybrid gold work which was just beginning to be produced. This emergent artistic tradition accurately reflects the *realpolitik* of relations between the two peoples: a convergence based on mutual advantage, sharply contrasting to both people's relations with the Persians, where mutual antagonism fuelled the desire for dominance and subjugation.

This is not to say, however, that the Greeks considered the Scythians to be their equals, or *vice versa.* The Scythian élite clearly considered the town-dwelling Greek traders and craftsmen as inferiors. For their part, the Greeks coined the term 'barbarian', referring to the 'babble' of the unintelligible languages of the steppe nomads. Herodotus makes it abundantly clear that by coming to the Black Sea he has reached the furthest outposts of the civilized world, with the aim of reporting what lay beyond. He was on the look-out for the exotic, and the Scythians certainly practised customs which seemed bizarre to the intrepid reporter.

Scythian ritual practices were markedly different from Greek, so Herodotus goes into great detail about them. So much so, in fact, that it is clear that he is relating the first-hand reports of people who have taken part in these rituals. In particular he singles out sacrifices to Ares which are carried out 'at the seat of government of every district' annually. Ares, the war god, is represented by an ancient iron sword. The sword is placed point-upwards on the top of a large heap of brushwood, and horses and cattle are sacrificed with it. Humans are sacrificed to it, too, but in a different way. The Scythians pick one in every hundred prisoners of war and:

Wine is poured on his head and his throat is cut over a bowl; the bowl is then carried to the top of the platform and the blood in it poured over the sword.

In a related ritual, Herodotus tells us that all Scythian warriors drink the blood of the first person they kill. The heads of all enemies killed in battle must be taken to the king and a warrior receives his share of the war booty on production of his 'receipt', his victim's head – 'no head, no loot'. The warrior then strips the scalp from the skull. He may choose to attach it to his bridle, or he may take several of them and stitch them together, to make a cloak out of them. He may also take his victim's skull and cut the top off, clean it out, then gild it, turning it into a golden drinking vessel which is only used on special ritual occasions.

This practice of cleaning and gilding skulls appears to have been extremely widespread: there are reliable reports of identical behaviour on the Chinese frontiers as well as among most of the nomad groups of the steppes. In some cases, the practice was not confined to enemy skulls – some groups are said to preserve the skulls of revered ancestors in the same way. So the importance of the skull-chalices seems to be that they are sacred objects, whatever their provenance. They may also have been used when two people wished to swear an oath. For this they would pour out some wine then mix a little of both parties' blood in it before drinking it together.

Here are a whole series of ritual events which have extremely powerful resonances in the Arthurian romances. Almost 1000 years before Arthur was purported to have lived, and nearly 2000 years before his tales were written down, one of the most powerful nations in the world believed in magical, divine swords, weapons closely associated with human blood and sacrifice. They carried the heads of their victims to the king; they then cut off the scalps of their victims and made cloaks from them, and liked to make golden cups for special ritual occasions.

Both Arthur and Lancelot have magic swords; human blood is repeatedly seen as having magical properties; the Damsel of the Cart brings a whole cartload of human heads to Arthur's court; twice Arthur is associated with cloaks and mantles made from human hair; the Holy Grail, though not normally associated with skulls, is certainly golden and constantly associated with blood and wine.

Although we assume that the blood–wine connection is a purely Christian tradition, here is evidence for the mystical linkage of the two substances more than 400 years before the birth of Christ. In fact, the inclusion of symbolically cannibalistic rituals (eating flesh and drinking blood) in the Christian canon seems decidedly anomalous in a credo otherwise dedicated to love and pacifism. It is certainly tempting to speculate that the entire Grail–gold–blood–wine motif is a very superficial Christian gloss on a much older and very widespread tradition, especially as the same linked symbolism was an important element in early Celtic ritual too.

The most complex rituals Herodotus describes are the funerary rites for kings and great leaders. These involve the mummification of the dead monarch and the progressing of his body throughout Scythia for a period of forty days before interment in a specially constructed house made of wooden poles. He is laid to rest with his treasures, notably gold cups, and his principal wife, servants and finest horses are all sacrificed and interred with him. Then the people raise a huge mound over the grave, called a *kurgan*, many of which can still be seen on the steppes to this day.

The procedures Herodotus describes have been corroborated in detail by archaeological findings, so there is no reason to doubt that the last act of the mortuary rites actually took place, although for obvious reasons physical evidence of the practice has not survived.

This final act took the following form: a year after the king's death, fifty of his finest servants were selected for the ritual. Herodotus is at pains to point out that those selected were not imported slaves, they were true-born Scythians, the king's most loyal subjects. They were all strangled and gutted, their bodies stuffed with chaff then sewn up again. Next, fifty of the king's finest horses were killed and stuffed in a similar manner. A series of fifty pairs of stakes were then driven into the ground in a circle surrounding the royal tomb mound. Fifty wheels broken in half were attached to the stakes, rims facing downwards and the dead horses were then placed on these 'stands' so that their legs dangled freely without touching the ground. Finally, the fifty sacrificed men, with poles thrust through them from top to bottom, were impaled on the horses, and when all were in place the mourners departed, leaving the ghostly cavalcade prancing round the grave of the king.

Herodotus offers us no explanation for this strange ritual of the 'merry-go-round of ghostly knights', although as the closing act in the terminal rite of passage it clearly symbolizes the protective ring of his principal vassals dispatched to follow the king into the afterlife. It is curious that these symbolic vassals should be arranged 'in the round', just as Arthur would arrange his knights at his famous round table.

Much of the rest of Herodotus's descriptions of the Scythians and their neighbours to the east is taken up with the practical details of who lived where. Among these descriptive passages, he tells us of a 'bald' people who have snub noses and long chins. This seems to be one of the very early references to people of Mongoloid appearance who, although not bald, are generally beardless. These people – who Herodotus plainly had no direct contact with – also seem to spend their winters in white felt tents arranged around trees or, more probably, using a lattice-like structure to support the tent, just as the nomads do today.

Elsewhere, Herodotus mentions that the Budini, whose town Gelonus was destroyed by Darius, all have blue-grey eyes and red hair. Interestingly, he points out that the townsfolk, however, do not look like their overlords, the Budini, and speak a language that is half-Scythian and half-Greek. Yet another example, then, of a mounted warrior élite imposing themselves on a local pedestrian population.

Another group which interests Herodotus are the Sauromatae. He recounts how a tribe of fierce warrior-women, the Amazons, were defeated by the Greeks but managed to escape and flee to Scythia. The Scythians were wary of the new arrivals at first, but soon some of their young men started liaisons with the women they called *Oeorpata*, which meant 'man-killer' in their language. These young men tried to persuade the warrior-women to come and live with them as their wives, but the Amazons thought they would never be accepted by the Scythian women. They declared:

> We are riders; our business is with the bow and the spear and we know nothing of women's work . . . your women stay at home in their waggons occupied with feminine tasks and never go out to hunt . . . we could not possibly agree.

They proposed instead that the young Scythians should accompany them on a trek eastward to find a place where they could set up on

their own. The men agreed to this and that was how the Sauroma-
tian people (later known as the Sarmatians) came to be:

> Ever since then the women of the Sauromatae have kept their
> old ways, riding to hunt on horseback sometimes with, some-
> times without their men, taking part in war and wearing the
> same sort of clothes as men. The language of these people is the
> Scythian, but it has always been a corrupt form of it because the
> Amazons were never able to learn to speak it properly. They
> have a marriage law which forbids a girl to marry until she has
> killed an enemy in battle; some of their women, unable to fulfil
> this condition, grow old and die unmarried.

Over the last two decades, a large number of Sarmatian graves have
been found to contain weapons – spear points, arrow heads, knives,
even a whetstone – and female skeletons. So, although the story of
the man-eating Amazons may be an exaggeration, there is little
doubt that some female Sarmatians really were women-warriors.
Given the men's predilection for disappearing for prolonged periods
on raiding parties, this female militarization seems both necessary
and predictable. Women martial artists, capable of both fighting and
doubtless teaching their own offspring to fight, is yet another theme
that is common to both the real cultures of the steppes and the
'fictive' culture of Arthurian legend.

To summarize, although doubtless some of the points of
convergence between Scythian reality and Arthurian fiction may be
coincidental, an increasing number of the more perplexing
elements in the fiction played a part in the real lives of the
Scythians: their magic swords, human-hair coats, golden chalices
for the consumption of blood–wine; queens who take heads and
bathe them in human blood; women – if they are not war-making

women-warriors – whose world centres on their carts and tents; old men who consider self-sacrifice the best way to end their lives; and deceased kings who arrange their prancing knights in a ghostly round table.

These people are not only *the* supreme horsemen and women, warrior-aristocrats who fight and dominate from the saddle, who love to set off on quests and adventures in pursuit of riches, power and encounters with the supernatural, even their most sacred ritual life enshrines such central concepts as the divine sword and the golden Holy Grail.

Given the uncannily high level of correlation between the real culture of the steppe nomads and the Arthurian fiction, it seems unlikely that this has come about coincidentally. Yet the two 'cultures' are separated by 2000 miles and nearly two millennia. As this is the case, there are two possible explanations for all these striking parallels. First, the two cultures may have descended from a common root culture, and therefore share the deep-seated motifs which appear in both Scythian ritual and Arthurian story-telling. And I suspect there is an element of truth in this view.

Both cultures were produced by Indo-European speaking peoples with common ethnic origins. There has been much debate about the form of this culture before the Indo-European Diaspora began, although this is mostly speculation. But we do know that some key words and certain ideas are very widespread among Indo-European speakers. The Grail-Cauldron motif is a good example of a widely diffused theme which was shared by Celtic, Germanic and Iranian-speaking peoples for at least 1000 years.

Likewise, the vision of water sources – springs, streams, lakes and bogs – as holy places is equally widespread. In keeping with the Celts and Germans, the Scythians also named specific springs 'Sacred Ways' according to Herodotus. But the magical powers of cooking pots and water sources are not confined to Indo-European mythic symbolism, they are found all over the world, and this is the problem with this approach. At this level we are dealing with symbols which have near-universal appeal and are, therefore, of little use when trying to pin down the exact provenance of specific ideas.

The other, potentially much more convincing approach is to see if we can actually map out a path – or paths – which cross the chasm of 2000 miles and 2000 years of history, tracing real connections linking the people of the steppes in classical times to the Arthurian story-tellers of medieval north-west Europe. The clues to finding these paths lie not only in the records of the Greeks and Romans, but in the wonderfully rich archaeological heritage the steppe nomads left behind them.

CHAPTER SIX

The Steppe World

HERODOTUS LEFT US A VITALLY IMPORTANT AND DETAILED PICTURE OF the nomads of the steppes and their early history which, given its antiquity, has proved to be extraordinarily accurate. But the picture he paints portrays only a very small portion of the totality of the nomads' world. His informants were of course living on the very westernmost edge of the lands of the nomads. Inevitably as he pressed them for information about who or what lay beyond the frontiers of their own experience and knowledge, 'facts' began to fudge and fuse with the fantastical.

This is an extremely widespread – perhaps universal – phenomenon. It is not just Scythians who have one-eyed people and gold-guarding griffins on the peripheries of their cultural horizons. The Chinese still refer to us as 'long-noses' and 'barbarians'; the Americans fear and distrust the Russian 'Reds'; and many British refer to Germans disparagingly as 'Huns', which, as we will shortly see, they most certainly are not. This last epithet is of course derived directly from the Graeco-Roman view of the world, where all those living outside of their immediate spheres of control were characterized as barbarians – uncivilized, threatening and repugnant. Herodotus himself was accused by some Athenians of being a 'savage-lover' for daring to counter the prejudices of the republican citizens with some of the real facts about the worlds at the borders of their vision and control.

At the time when Herodotus's adventures took him first to ancient Egypt then up to the Black Sea, in the mid-fifth century BC, nobody in the classical world knew that another complex, literate society existed even further to the east of the lands of the nomads, in China. The nomads knew it and were in contact with the Chinese, sometimes in a friendly way, sometimes not. In the centuries following Herodotus's days, known to scholars as the period of 'trade or raid', these interactions became so intense that, on the one hand the Chinese regularly sent huge bribes of silk, fine objects of art and even royal princesses to the nomads; on the other, they also regularly tried to drive them away from their frontiers and built a succession of Great Walls to keep them out.

The nomads most frequently in contact with the Chinese, who consistently presented the greatest military threat, were called the Hsiung-Nu by the Chinese. This may be something of a blanket term, rather as the Greeks used the term 'Scythian' for almost all of the nomads in contact with the classical world. Most experts believe that the Hun – the most successful of the invaders of Europe under Attila – were Hsiung-Nu, but I am not convinced about this peculiarly poorly researched connection. The relevant point is that by the last centuries before Christ, the nomads (Hsiung-Nu) had virtually encircled the western and northern borders of China, and in some places had penetrated the Chinese homelands.

If, in those days, you were travelling eastward across the steppes on a horse, there were only a limited number of places where you could cross the mountains and deserts which isolate China and south-east Asia from the rest of the continent (see map, page 234–5). You could 'get in' by crossing into the western end of the Taklamakan desert from what is now Tajikistan, via Samarkand. You could then skirt to the north or south of the desert, following the line of oases which run around its peripheries. Once you reached the eastern end of the desert you could travel relatively easily down the Gansu Corridor into the heart of China. The second route in is a little to the north of this, where you could ride through the Djungarian Gates from Khazakhstan, keeping the Tien Shan mountains to your south and the Altai mountains to your north. Following the northern edge of the Tien Shan you would skirt the westernmost extension of the Gobi desert before cutting south to join up with the previous route and heading down the Gansu Corridor to China proper. These two east–west routes would become the famed Silk Road by about AD 100.

Alternatively, if you kept trekking north-east on the steppes, leaving the Altai mountains to your south, you would come to south-west Siberia. There is no way through the mountains to your south until you come to the bottom of Lake Baikal. Here a narrow pass cuts southwards, letting you into Mongolia. If you cross the Mongolian Gobi you will come to a fertile region of northern China where the great Huang He river scribes a huge arch, known as the Ordos Bend. This is the third way into China.

If you did not cut south at Lake Baikal, you would have to keep travelling a little north of east, the mountains preventing you from turning south until you came to the headwaters of the Heilong Jiang river. You could follow this river down into Manchuria in north-east China.

By 200 BC, the Hsiung-Nu had taken all four of these routes;

their presence is clearly visible both in the Chinese records and in archaeological remains. So by that date the lands of the nomads of the steppes stretched from the Black Sea almost to the Pacific, maybe 4000 miles. The Hsiung-Nu's territory alone extended to around 2000 miles from west to east.

The Hsiung-Nu were apparently both ethnically and linguistically distinct from the nomads living to their west. They spoke languages from the Altaic language family, mother tongue of the Turkic-speaking peoples and not Indo-European. They were mostly Mongoloid in appearance, although on their western borders they were of mixed ethnic stock, probably through intermarriage with the Iranian-speaking steppe nomads. Yet despite these sharp ethnic and linguistic differences, the culture of the Hsiung-Nu was extraordinarily similar to their neighbours to the west. They too were fierce mounted warriors living in tents and carts, herding their flocks and lording it over the pockets of farmers who lived in the more fertile, well-watered parts of their domains. They had their own kings and a complex politico-military hierarchy which meant that they could put 50–100,000 well co-ordinated cavalrymen into the field if necessary. Although the Chinese both feared and loathed them, they also admired their equestrian skills and their horses, and constantly sought to get hold of good breeding stock of the 'Heavenly horses of Fergana'.

The Hsiung-Nu's lifestyles, dress, weaponry, saddlery, harnessing and personal and equestrian adornments were all extraordinarily similar to those of their Iranian cousins living to their west. Their artistic aspirations were clearly moulded within the overall style of the steppe nomads known as the 'animal' style.

The 'animal' style seems to originate with the steppe nomads and it was certainly developed to the level of a truly fine art by artisans controlled by the nomads, if not the nomads themselves. Its earliest forms portray single animals, or pairs, and occasionally whole groups of animals. Curiously, the animals depicted are more frequently wild animals than the domesticates the nomads herded. When two or three animals are depicted they are nearly always a prey species being attacked by one or more predators.

It is never difficult to recognize the species of animal portrayed, but this is not to say that the art is representative; it is nearly all highly stylized. The intention of this styling appears to be to capture the movements of the animals and to feel the power which emanates from them. In this endeavour, the best pieces of Scythian gold work are supremely successful, achieving a level of artistic expression which ranks alongside the finest works of art produced anywhere in the world.

From a purely aesthetic point of view, the animal style has been seen by many experts as containing the most refined distillation of animal motion ever achieved. I agree and see it as *prima facie* evidence that the steppe nomads were not savages and barbarians but highly sophisticated people who achieved an extremely subtle perception of the world of nature which surrounded them. Had they been literate (something peculiarly hard to achieve and retain in nomadic societies) I have little doubt that their culture would have gone down in history as one of the most important of all the 'ancient civilizations' of the Old World.

At the beginning of the eighteenth century, the Russian Tsar Peter the Great was one of the first people to recognize the extraordinary artistic ability of the early steppe nomads. Robbing the tombs of the Scythians in the heart of their great raised earth mounds – *kurgans* – was something of a national sport in those days, but as more and more brilliant pieces arrived in St Petersburg the tsar issued an edict instructing his local representatives to buy up all the robbed art they could lay their hands on and bring it to the capital. In this way, he amassed a vast collection of superb works of art which are still housed in the Hermitage museum, St Petersburg, for all to marvel at.

Further impressive evidence of the steppe nomads' extraordinary sophistication came to light some two centuries later, when Peter's collection was complemented by some of the most spectacular archaeological finds of the century. A Soviet ethnologist, Sergei Rudenko, had been working with the Kazhak nomads for many years in south-west Siberia before he decided to investigate some of the huge funeral mounds which were scattered along a valley that the Kazhaks called Pazyryk.

In 1929, Rudenko set off on horseback to this remote valley with a team of excavators and began to dig in the nearly permanently frozen ground. He returned there again some twenty years later and excavated a further four large *kurgans*. All of them had been looted, in most cases shortly after they were sealed up, and we can assume that all the major golden objects were stolen by the tomb-robbers. Yet despite this, the finds in the tombs amounted to a vast cultural treasure trove. The tombs had been dug in the very brief season when the permafrost thaws in this part of Siberia and had frozen shortly after interment. This meant that the state of preservation of practically all the objects placed in the tombs, from human remains, sacrificed horses, clothes, wooden objects, carpets, wall-hangings, cups, hats, beakers, boots, stools and tables, horse saddles and harnesses, ceramics, even food – and a myriad more sacred and profane objects – were almost perfectly preserved in the ice.

The people who made these tombs clearly believed in sending their male and female leaders, warriors and the like, into the afterlife very well kitted out for an extended stay, and just about everything except their (looted) gold was still in the tombs. In many ways, because they cast such extraordinarily detailed light on a hitherto little known culture, these discoveries were even more important than those made in Egypt just a few years earlier in 1922 – when the boy-king Tutankhamun's undisturbed tomb was uncovered. But because the tombs came to light in Stalinist Soviet Russia they were not brought to the attention of the rest of the world until Rudenko's book on the excavations was published in English in 1970.

Rudenko himself dated the Pazyryk tombs to 500–300 BC, but recent revision of the material suggests that they may be a little younger, probably 400–200 BC. The valley itself is in south-west Siberia just north of the Altai mountains, in what is probably the most isolated and worst documented part of all of central Asia, virtually unknown to the classical world far away to the west and separated from the Chinese world by two formidable mountain ranges. In this sense, the incredible wealth of the contents of the tombs is that much more mind-boggling.

In the tombs there were imported Persian carpets, one of them edged with locally mined gold and fur from the Arctic; there was cheetah fur and coriander seeds from the Near East, as well as many representations of lions; there were silver and bronze mirrors from China and much Chinese silk, some of it clearly embroidered locally with images of goddesses and European-like mounted warriors on finely bred race horses. By this time, the imagery brought back from Assyria by the Scythians had already fused with the indigenous 'animal' style, producing magnificently fluid images of many species of monsters. Griffins, sphinxes – and a myriad of composite mythical beasts – are found superbly worked in wood, leather, silk and felt appliqué alongside real beasts such as tigers, leopards and wolves.

In all, Rudenko found more than 1100 objects in these five tombs, as well as several human and horse mummies. He was immediately struck by how precisely Herodotus's descriptions of Scythian culture in general and funerary traditions in particular were borne out by the tombs' contents. So many of the elements that I isolated in Chapter Five, in relation to the Arthurian canon, receive corroboration in the Pazyryk tombs. There are also some extremely interesting tie-ins which were not revealed by Herodotus.

The people in the tombs were apparently of ethnically mixed stock, some Mongoloid, others Caucasoid. Subsequent excavations in this region confirm this pattern of ethnic mixing. Situated as they were, on the western edge of Hsiung-Nu territory and the eastern borders of the Iranian (Caucasoid) lands, it makes sense that the population would be mixed here. One of the men, called 'the chief' by Rudenko, was extremely tall – about 6ft 3in (1.90 metres). He was an old man who evidently died in battle. He had several axe or sword wounds on his body and had been scalped. His allies had evidently retaken his body and maybe even had recovered his scalp, as his skull is covered, but the Russians have not tested the skin and hair to see if it is human or a piece of horse skin sewn on to cover the scalping. Another young man, found much more recently, had evidently died from a massive sword-cut to the belly. So these people were certainly warriors, scalpers, and very probably head-takers (elsewhere in Scythian territory headless bodies have been found in graves and there are images of Scythian men carrying taken heads).

Some of the men have stubbly beards but others, like many Mongoloid peoples, do not. A very interesting item found in one tomb is a false beard. It was hung across the mummy's face on a string looped over each ear. On some of the fairly rare depictions of human faces the men all have beards which follow the same line as the false beard did – that is, they grow down the sides of the cheeks and across the chin under the mouth, but leave the entire mouth and upper lip area clean shaven (or uncovered). As other Scythian art nearly always depicts men with beards, we can safely assume that these were a sign of prestige and dignity – perhaps to the point where those who were genetically unable to grow them, donned false ones. Conversely, we can assume that the cutting of a man's beard was a humiliation, especially if it was forced, as in the Arthurian legends.

An unexpected aspect of the human Pazyryk mummies is that many of them, both men and women, have tattoos. These generally depict magnificently antlered deer (an extremely popular symbol throughout Scythia) and fierce composite predators – beasts such as griffins and flying eagle-headed lions attacking their prey.

We know from the variety of furs found in the tombs that the Pazyryk were dedicated hunters, and it is quite likely that they, along with many of the other steppe nomads, considered hunting from their horses to be a pleasurable pastime as well as a source of meat and furs. There are very close connections between hunting and martial skills, especially if both are performed on horseback. The Scythians were renowned as archers who could shoot with great accuracy from their galloping horses – the precise skill needed for killing game from the saddle. Similarly, hunting deer or wild boar with lances or spears requires near-identical weapons skills as those used when charging infantry.

Hunting may also have been of economic importance as furs from this area were highly prized and important trade goods. That hunting was the preserve of the mounted warrior élite is alluded to several times in the written records of the Scythians, and appears to be corroborated by the tattoos and bodily ornaments worn by the ruling classes. The Arthurian legends certainly continue this tradition, with royal hunts a regular feature of many of the tales and hunting a prerogative of the ruling classes, as indeed it still is in today's Great Britain.

Like all the other Scythians, the Pazyryk sacrificed horses when they buried their leaders, and luckily some of the stable-tombs escaped the attentions of the grave-robbers. When Rudenko unearthed them, several contained quite well-preserved horse mummies as well as decayed skeletons. Rudenko himself knew plenty about horses because he had spent several years with the nomadic Kazhaks at a time when the only way to get around Siberia was on horseback. Examining the mummified animals, he soon realized that most of them were fine quality thoroughbred horses, riding mounts, not draught animals. But even more impressive than the breeding were the elaborately decorated harnesses. Saddle cloths, bridles, chest and nose plates, even cheek pieces, were all adorned with a huge array of designs in the animal style. However, most interesting from our point of view were the elaborate head-dresses worn by many of the horses.

These were placed over the bridles and encased much of the horse's head, rather in the way 'plumed' horse were used to draw funeral carriages in Victorian times. But the Pazyryk head-dresses were not feathered, they were antlered. Evidently the Pazyryk took delight in converting their finest horses into deer-horses. There are several examples of head-dresses with full-sized gilded antlers, and other examples of helmet-like head pieces with a deer's head mounted on the top.

It is tempting to combine these finds with a magnificent discovery from Tomb 5, the tomb of the scalped 'chief'. Here, Rudenko unearthed the well-preserved remains of an extremely finely made four-wheeled wooden carriage, one of the best-preserved ancient wooden vehicles ever found. Herodotus tells us that when a great chief or king died, his mummified body would be ceremonially paraded all round Scythia in a cart before being interred in his final resting place, the *kurgan*. The Scythians apparently believed that this period – the time of the 'living dead' – was an essential phase in the post-mortem process for guaranteeing the immortality of the deceased.

As I have mentioned, the motif of immortal figures travelling in a cart, drawn by stags, occurs in the Arthurian legends and is closely linked with the taking of heads in the *Perlesvaus*, one of the French versions of the tales. Linking the cart with the deer is admittedly speculative, but there can be no doubt that the Pazyryk and all the other Scythians held deer in such esteem that they frequently represented them in artistic form and strived to make their most prized possessions – their horses – resemble them.

As in ancient Egypt and many other early cultures, Rudenko's findings revealed that the Scythians created a world in miniature for their dead ancestors. Besides the horses, servants, wives and other attendants were sacrificed at the time of interment, and the burial chambers were fitted out with all the material goods used in the world of the living, even food. The tomb itself was lined with wooden poles, like a log cabin. This may well reflect the winter housing used by the Pazyryk. It is of course extremely cold in the Siberian winter, and today's nomads in the region pass the winter in mud and timber houses in sheltered valleys, only reverting to tents in summer. But the houses I have seen in the Altai mountains are constructed and furnished very much as if they are simply larger versions of the summer felt tents, or *yurts*. This may well have been the case when the Pazyryk lived in the valleys just to the north of the Altai.

Then, as today, the walls of the houses (and tents) were lined with superbly worked decorative wall-hangings, the floors covered by carpets and mats; they had raised platforms as beds, also covered with cloths and cushions. Given that everything had to be transportable there was no bulky furniture, but they did have small stools and tables. One particularly fine table had four removable legs, each carved in the form of a leaping feline. On the tables were wooden bowls, leather flasks, drinking horns and the like.

The Scythian household interior, therefore, shared many characteristics with medieval north-west European households, where the (stone or mud) walls were hung with tapestries, the floor dotted with rugs or carpets and bed platforms covered with quilts, pillows and coverlets. There is even a reference in Chrétien de Troyes's *Arthurian Romances* to Arthur possessing a fine pair of folding stools, each with four legs, two carved in the form of leaping leopards, the other two as crocodiles. Later in the same work Chrétien gives a description of Arthur setting out with his court:

> You should have seen all the bedclothes, coverlets and cushions being packed, trunks filled, packhorses loaded, the many carts and wagons piled high – for they did not skimp on the number of tents, pavilions and shelters: a wise clerk could not write down in a day all the equipment and provisions that were ready instantly. The king set off from Caerleon as if he were going off to war, followed by all his barons; not a single maiden stayed behind, as the queen brought them all for pomp and dignity.

Having myself seen an entire Kazhak village pack up and move to their summer pastures, the parallels with the Arthurian description are uncanny. There is no doubt that a Scythian herding group on the move would have been extremely similar. This medieval European/Scythian model of the mobile household certainly bears no resemblance to Roman households, whether in Italy or Britain, with their mosaics, underfloor heating and classical architecture. It seems very clear that the domestic furnishings of Middle Age Europe owe their origins far more closely to the steppes than they do to the classical world.

The same is true of the appearance and dress of the Scythians. Whereas the Romans and Greeks were small in stature and dark in complexion, the Scythians were tall, fair-skinned, and mostly had blond or red hair and blue or green eyes. The Greeks and Romans wore loose-fitting lightweight clothes and sandals while the Scythians wore belted tunics, tight-fitting trousers and capes or mantles and boots, all of course clothes adapted for life in the saddle. While the Greeks and Romans wore their hair short, often depicted in tight curls, and were clean-shaven, the Scythians are invariably depicted with full beards and long straight hair. Sometimes their heads are covered with a pointed woollen or leather hat which follows the line of the sides of the face and probably fastened under the chin.

By the fifth century BC, this pointed cap – along with their recurved bows – had become the 'trademarks' of the Scythians. Their fame had evidently reached at least as far as Italy, where a beautiful Etruscan wine serving bowl is decorated with four statuettes of mounted archers with pointed hats on prancing horses, two of them shooting their recurved bows forwards, the other two firing backwards in the classic Scythian posture. Greek vases and urns also depict mounted archers with the tell-tale pointed hats and recurved bows firing backwards. One particular piece is especially revealing: it depicts a centaur, half-man, half-horse. Centaurs first appear in Greek art in the fifth-century BC, just when the Greeks were getting to know the Scythians. Being only semi-human, creatures like the centaur and satyr (man-goat) are seen as demarcators of the culture–nature boundary – the human 'us' combined with the animal 'other'.

In images such as those on the Parthenon, the centaurs are straightforward man-horses who get drunk and try to carry off the Greeks' womenfolk. But a large wine-mixing bowl, made in Athens in 580 BC, gives a much more culturally specific rendering of a centaur named Chiron. He is man at the front, horse at the back, but is also clearly an archer. In his right hand he holds the classic recurved Scythian bow and over his left shoulder is a pole bedecked with six hares that he has shot. He also has a large bushy beard.

Herodotus tells us of the Scythians' passion for hare-coursing, which leaves little doubt that the centaur is ethnically a Scythian. Interestingly, though, this centaur, unlike his generally drunken lecherous fellows, is married, immortal, a skilled hunter and a healer. In Greek myths he is tutor to the heroes Achilles and Hercules. Perhaps in providing all these positive attributes to Chiron, the Greeks were covertly acknowledging the talents of some Scythians, while caricaturing centaurs in general as wine-loving lecherous barbarians. Either way it seems that by the fifth century BC, Scythian equestrian skills were so widely acknowledged that to give a Scythian flavour to an immortal horse-man seemed appropriate.

Two other images that are closely associated in Greek minds with the steppe nomads concern women. Classical Greece fostered the first wholly chauvinistic society that we have records of, and it was of course largely copied by its successors in the Roman Empire. The Greeks and Romans excluded women from virtually all forms of political and economic responsibility, and even drastically restricted their socializing, both within and across the sex barrier. They were, therefore, both shocked and intrigued by the barbarian snake-woman goddess and the barbarian man–woman warriors, the Amazons.

The founding of the nation through the coupling of a Greek hero (who has appropriately had his horses pinched) with a divine snake-woman who holds the hero captive for as long as she can, clearly appealed to the Oedipal Greek psyche. Consequently her image is to be found in many of the Greek-Scythian settlements around the Black Sea, as well as on Scythian jewellery, perhaps reminding the Scythians of female authority while reassuring the Greeks that female power can be overcome.

The Greek psyche seems to be appeased by the second iconic Scythian image, the Amazons, as their story begins with their military defeat by the Greeks. But the Amazons then escape into Scythia where the warrior-women mate with local young men and create a new hybrid people, the Sauromatiae (later known as the Sarmatians). But here the two stories of Scythian half-women diverge, because while the snake-woman remains safely in the realms of mythology, Sarmatian women-warriors were real, and by the fourth century BC they and their men were beginning to make their presence felt around the Black Sea. The Sarmatians, with their women-warriors, were already pressing the Scythians westwards and thus coming into direct contact with the Greeks. They must, therefore, have presented a threat to the Greeks, both physically and as a challenge to their own 'civilized' yet wholly chauvinistic socio-sexual orientation. That this threat was real is illustrated by a spectacular find in the city of Rostov, where the river Don flows into the sea of Azov.

There, in 1988, a young Russian archaeologist discovered an undisturbed grave whose contents ring so many Arthurian bells that it is worth quoting them in detail. The grave was of a young Sarmatian woman, aged about twenty, who had died in the second century AD. Her head was crowned with a gold diadem decorated with stags, birds and trees. She wore bracelets and a ring, and beside her lay an axe and horse-harnesses. Around her neck she wore a huge golden collar, decorated all over with magical beasts – dragons fighting what appear to be eagle-headed warriors. At the centre of the collar a beautifully fashioned golden man sat cross-legged, his hair and beard carefully groomed, a sword across his lap, and in his hands he held a ceremonial cup.

The imagery surrounding this wondrous Sarmatian warrior-priestess is all magical, and all the magic is found in the Arthurian tales – magic stags, trees, dragons and monsters, and a man meditating with magic sword and cup who could almost be Merlin himself.

Another of the most famous pieces of Scythian gold work is also replete with Arthurian themes. To be able to read it properly one need only know that in any area of dry plains in the world – be they in central Asia, Africa or North or South America – trees only grow near to water sources. A superb gold plaque in Peter the Great's collection, dating from the fourth to second centuries BC, depicts two horses, saddled but resting in the shade of a tree. Their reins are held by a squire who sits quietly in the background. In the foreground a noble's bow case *cum* quiver hangs in the branches of the tree and the warrior lies on the ground, his head cradled in the lap of a finely dressed woman wearing a magnificent tall conical hat. Is the warrior sleeping or dying? We cannot tell, though every time I look at this wonderfully expressive and moving piece I hear Malory's words from the ultimate climax of *Le Morte D'Arthur*:

'Now put me into the barge' said the king.
    And he did so softly; and there received him three queens with great mourning; and so they set them down, and in one of their laps King Arthur laid his head.

Here the ladies of the lake come to soothe and comfort the dying king; there the noble lady cradles her man's head in the shade of the watery tree deep in the land of the steppes.

The Scythians posed another challenge to the Greek psycho-sexual order in the form of women-men, the Enarees. A fifth-century BC Greek manuscript, *Airs, Waters and Places*, claims that Scythian male fertility was low (as I mentioned in the previous chapter) because of their custom of wearing tight-fitting trousers and the constant jolting their genitalia received in the saddle, coupled with their lack of interest in fondling themselves. Some scholars have recently affirmed that tight trousers and saddle-joggling may indeed reduce fertility, but whatever the objective basis, there is clear evidence that some Scythian men became transvestites and acquired the power of prophecy and other shamanic abilities by abandoning their masculinity.

By giving up their natal sex these men may also have been able to prolong their lives, by not dying in battle. Either way, the simple equation is that neutering marks an alteration in status from active warrior to passive shaman/elder. And a similar process takes place repeatedly in the Arthurian legends when 'maimed kings' surrender their potency in old age to make way for young virile replacements.

So, in all these aspects of socio-sexual relations, there are echoes of Arthurian themes as well as direct correlations of specific imagery – snake-women, women-warriors, and castrated elders. These shared themes somehow seem to have crossed the powerful cultural and military barriers of the chauvinistic classical worlds of Greece and Rome.

They were not, however, carried there by the Scythians. Their demise has never been clearly documented, but it seems to be due to a series of different pressures. Although they are reported by Herodotus as being fiercely loyal to and protective of their own culture and customs, constant contact with the Greeks does seem to have eroded their independence of spirit.

Some of the greatest gold work found in their tombs gives us wonderful visions of the Scythian pastoral way of life. There are beautiful depictions of men handling their horses, hobbling them, leading them, teaching them to kneel so that a fallen warrior in armour would be able to remount. There are people milking mares and sheep, and men cleaning fleeces, all wrought in gold and thus extraordinarily reminiscent of Jason's golden fleece. There are also wonderfully serene portraits of men relaxing together, chatting, taking care of each other, and even one depiction of two men drinking together simultaneously from a single drinking horn. They are almost certainly drinking a mix of their own blood and wine, becoming blood-brothers.

These deeply intimate golden studies of pairs of men resonate with a very powerful and simple theme – Scythian men bonded very closely, swore to protect each other in combat or die in the process. On one beaker alone, we see one man trying to fix his 'brother's' toothache, his hand in his partner's mouth; the next depiction shows one man winding a bandage round the shin of his male partner, while in the third set two men lean on their spears chatting to each other with happy, smiling faces. Here is Scythian life in the quick, but it is not executed in the animal style. The quality of the work is breathtakingly fine, but the style is entirely representational – surely the work of Greek, or at least Greek-trained, craftsmen.

So, although they may have resisted it, by Herodotus's days the Scythians were gradually being drawn into the Greek world. The Greeks paid them handsomely for their grain, furs, fish, slaves and gold, and offered them the means to spend their wealth on wine, oil and works of fine art, mostly rendered in gold. City life was easily affordable for the dominant élite and may eventually, despite their proud nomadic past, have offered a greater draw than life in the saddle. At the same time the pressure from the east seems to have increased sharply in the third century BC, a time of cooler drier weather in central Asia. The Sarmatians, seasoned and tempered both in battle and by the herding way of life, put constant pressure on the Scythians.

We know next to nothing of the actual conflicts which took place, but we do know that by about 200 BC the Sarmatians dominated much of the territory once exclusively roamed by the Scythians. Being of extremely similar ethnic, linguistic and cultural stock, this process may not have involved much conflict. The militarily tougher Sarmatians, with their warrior-wives, may well have demanded and received submission from individual Scythian leaders in return for retaining control of some of their lands or the farm people they dominated – I have already mentioned the many subtle ways the steppe nomads devised to gain control over other peoples, and there is no doubt that they played these games among each other.

Caught between the Greeks to the west and south, and the Sarmatians to the east, Scythian society slipped quietly off the Eurasian stage around 200 BC. But their rather abrupt disappearance does raise the question of what, exactly, their society consisted of? We know, for example, that the Scythian rulers intermarried with each other, but they also intermarried with neighbours such as the Thracians. Although wealth certainly helped, social standing was to a large degree dependent on martial ability. This was how the élite arose from their particular familial and 'tribal' groupings. So perhaps the people who bore the name Scythian (and Sarmatian or Alan for that matter) were only the warrior élite, a dispersed embryonic aristocracy, capable of coming together in times of conflict but easily absorbed under other ethnic labels if their own failed.

In short, perhaps it only took a few strong Sarmatians to defeat a few weaker Scythians (perhaps in single combat, their favourite trial of strength), then a few deft marriage alliances, perhaps an expulsion or two, to turn a former Scythian domain into a province where Sarmatian rule prevailed. Certainly this would have been followed by an influx of family and kin of the victorious Sarmatians, but it did not necessarily entail the wholesale expulsion of the Scythians or the farming populations they dominated. In fact, as one entire section of Scythian society was known as the 'agricultural Scythians', it seems certain that the Sarmatians would want to keep these people on the land and merely rename them 'farming Sarmatians'.

So, in reality, remarkably few heads had to roll – and not many names needed to be changed on the roll-call – for 'Sarmatians' to replace 'Scythians'. A further reason for the facility of this transition was that the two groups were culturally homogenous. Cimmerians, Massagetae, Scythians, Sarmatians shared the same basic lifestyle and outlook, and held many key elements of their cultures in common. The evidence we have suggests strongly that they recognized the same pantheon, which included the war god represented by the sacred sword, that their supernatural paragon included much the same composite beasts, and that the same weight was given to hunting, fighting and martial prowess as the Scythians recognized. This high level of cultural continuity is extremely important. That people with different names should share ideas and practices over an enormous area and a large time-span helps us in a big way, because the reporting of these peoples is very varied.

I have presented a great deal of information about the fifth-century BC Scythians because we have good data about them which matches the archaeological record. We can trust this stuff. The same cannot be said for the available data nearer to the period which interests us, that is the first centuries after Christ. But the fact that we can see a strong cultural 'descent line' or pedigree means that we can say with some degree of safety 'If the Scythians did it or thought it, or believed it, then it is likely that their successors the Sarmatians and the Alans did it or knew it too'.

Not that these groups were identical – there is one very key way in which the Sarmatians differed from the Scythians. This lay in their arms and weaponry. Where the Scythians' fame lay with their archery, the Sarmatians were swordsmen. They used long slashing swords delivering blows at close quarters from the saddle. They used bows and arrows, too, but had discovered that with a big slashing sword a cavalryman could close for the fight and literally cut people down. Where exactly they got this idea from we do not know, but interestingly it may have come from Celts living in Eastern Europe at this time, great craftsmen who specialized in the production of long swords.

Several Celtic swords have been found in Sarmatian graves. But it was certainly the Sarmatians who recognized the potential of these weapons. They continued to use spears which could either be thrown or used as a lance, but it is relatively easy for an infantryman to block, parry or pull a spear free from a mounted attacker. Not so the long sword with its honed double-cutting edges. Easy to manipulate in one hand (leaving the other free to hold a shield or steer a horse), impossible for the opponent to grasp and delivering massive force when wielded from above, the long sword is the ideal weapon for those really wishing to do mounted battle at close quarters. Without a shadow of doubt the Sarmatians' long swords were superior to the short *akinake* Scythian sword, and the Roman infantry would learn painfully how useless their stubby little stabbing swords were against the great sword swipes of the barbarians.

Clearly illustrated on Trajan's column in Rome, the Sarmatians also wore scale armour and even protected their horses with it. Prior to this, various other types of armour were quite common. But most of it was made either as plate armour, as the Romans and Greeks wore, or leather armour to which discs or rings made of horn, iron or precious metals, such as gold or silver, were sewn. These latter styles of armour may look spectacular and offer some protection, but plate armour greatly restricts movement and leaves areas around the joints of the body vulnerable to attack. Scale armour does not restrict movement and gives better protection over more of the body.

These two technical innovations certainly gave the Sarmatians the edge over their enemies and allowed them to develop the tactics associated with heavy cavalry, where a wall of horsemen charges straight at the enemy infantry lines, smashing their ranks and forcing them to scatter. Where light cavalry were very effective for harassing the enemy and running them down once they broke ranks, heavy cavalry were real shock troops, the panzer divisions of their day.

The one element the Sarmatians initially lacked to complete their mastery of heavy cavalry tactics was the stirrup. As well as improving overall balance (hence accuracy) and stability, in specifically military terms the stirrup will keep a cavalryman in his saddle if he deploys his lance at the end of his charge. Without stirrups, if you strike a rigidly fixed object – a shield or the body of an infantryman or opposing cavalryman – you will be ejected backwards off your horse. Stirrups allow you to counter the impact by 'braking' with your legs. It seems likely that Scythian warriors had been using leather straps attached to their saddles to help them mount, but the Sarmatians were certainly using solid stirrups by the third century AD. The idea for the stirrup may in fact have originated in China, where an image of a cavalryman with a stirrup dates from the eighth century BC.

Long swords, flexible armour and the stirrup – all three of these developments are, of course, essential prerequisites for the pursuit of the ritual and real warfare practices which fill the pages of the Arthurian canon, from joust and tourney to single combat and all-out war.

The Romans quite quickly grasped the merits of long swords for cavalrymen and brought them into their own armies, but they were fatally slow in adopting the latter two developments – errors of judgement which, as we shall see, ultimately cost them their empire.

We have already seen that Sarmatian women took a much more active part in political and military life than their predecessors. They were of course mothers and rearers of children, whose domestic life centred around their tents and wagons, but they were also free to hunt and fight if they chose. Evidence from graves confirms that warrior-women did not necessarily give up the female aspects of their lives, as many are buried with both weapons and mirrors, make-up kits, spindles and other specifically feminine objects. Mirrors were not just used for face-gazing in those days, they were also magical objects in the hands of shamanesses and priestesses. Sarmatian women certainly maintained the ancient religious traditions of the steppe-dwellers, acting as both diviners and sacrificers, as well as quite probably healers and fortune-tellers.

This involvement of women in all aspects of social life once again both distinguishes the Sarmatians from their Greek and Roman counterparts, and places Sarmatian reality very much in line with the fiction of the Arthurian world. It also, incidentally, links these steppe women with a specific medieval esoteric tradition. There is plenty of evidence that steppe women-priestesses liked to wear tall conical hats with brims at the base, identical, in fact, with the hats supposedly worn by witches in the Dark Ages.

In the fields of art and decoration the Sarmatians continued to adhere to the animal style, making jewellery, belt buckles and the like in the form of real or magical animals, although their taste seems less elegant than that of the Scythians. The Sarmatians preferred their artwork heavily encrusted with stones in bright colours, and much of their art seems coarser than the Scythian heritage. None the less, it is unquestionably in the same tradition. If anything, though, Sarmatian art work seems to have been influenced by the Far East and China, whereas the Scythians were clearly inspired by the artwork of the Near East. Where Scythian art exudes the image of the griffin above all other magical beasts, the Sarmatians, like the young warrior princess found outside Rostov, tended to place the dragon at the pinnacle of their mystical paragon.

In fact, the very name 'Sarmatian' means 'lizard people'. In classical times, lizards, snakes and dragons were all considered to be much the same, especially when the label implied a symbolic, even totemic connection between the beast and a particular people. This epithet may indeed have come about through the Sarmatians' use of a very particular battle standard, consisting of a silken windsock sewn into the shape of a serpentine dragon which hissed when it filled with air as its bearer charged into battle. Remember that in 1130, Geoffrey of Monmouth portrayed Arthur's battle standard and his helmet crest as the dragon. It may be coincidence, maybe not, that a famous French illustrated manuscript from AD 1290 depicts king Arthur in pitched battle immediately beneath an exact reproduction of a Sarmatian dragon battle standard (see cover).

As mentioned, the Sarmatians gradually displaced the Scythians in the Black Sea area during the last centuries BC, but events which lay way outside their immediate control were also coming to bear on them. Far to the east, the power of the Hsiung-Nu had grown steadily, so much so that in 218 BC the Chinese completed the first of the Great Walls designed to keep them out. But in the following fifty years the Hsiung-Nu succeeded in dislodging at least one large group of Iranian-speaking pastoralists (the Chinese called them the Yueh Chi) from a key access point, the Gansu Corridor. This led to a wholesale evacuation westwards, and the 'domino effect' led to the Massagetae putting pressure on the Sarmatians' eastern frontiers.

Meanwhile to the west and south, the Mediterranean nations were also in turmoil. In Herodotus's lifetime an approximate equilibrium had been established between the four big players in the Mediterranean – the Greeks, Etruscans, Phoenicians and Carthaginians. But as the fifth century progressed, the people of the city of Rome broke free of Etruscan control and began to expand, first within Italy, then further afield. By 240 BC, the Romans had consolidated their hold on mainland Italy and had annexed Sicily, Corsica and Sardinia. In the following century they took control of much of Spain, North Africa and the Balkans. By 140 BC, competition between the nation states of the Mediterranean had been replaced by the almost total domination of the Roman super-state.

Although Greece remained nominally independent for some time, it soon succumbed to Roman domination, and by AD 14 the Romans had effectively redrawn the map of Europe, using the rivers Danube and Rhine as a means of bisecting the continent from the Black Sea to the North Sea, leaving the 'barbarians' to the north and east on the outside, and enclosing the 'civilized' Romans and their subjects on the inside. This enormous physical and ideological barrier would mark and scar the hearts and minds of all those living on either side of it, creating a legacy which has moulded both the history and the thinking of the peoples of western Eurasia ever since.

The nomads living closest to the new frontier were a sub-group of the Sarmatians known as the Iazyges, although the Romans only ever bothered to call them Sarmatians. They had moved into the steppe along the lower Dneister in the early second century BC. Their initial contacts with the Romans were not unfriendly and the frontier remained calm. There were some minor incursions and raids to and fro in the early decades of the new millennium, and as usual the nomads busied themselves making alliances with local sedentary kingdoms, fighting for those they deemed most likely to succeed. Some detachments of their cavalry fought alongside allies of the Romans in local skirmishes, and in AD 85–88 they fought for the Roman emperor Trajan in his wars against the Dacians. Pitted against them were their own cousins, the Sarmatian Roxolani, who were fighting in the pay of the Dacian king. Trajan eventually won and rewarded the Iazyges well. Their defeated cousins, the Roxolani, appear on the famous Trajan's column, dressed in full-scale armour tunics and trousers, their horses also heavily armoured, firing their recurved bows backwards from the saddle in the classic Scythian style.

Just four years later, however, the Iazyges made their first raid across the Danube and pillaged the Roman province of Moesia. They attacked once again in AD 105, this time having allied with the Roxolani, laying the kingdom of Dacia to waste. They were eventually beaten off by the emperor Hadrian, who made a peace treaty with them which was to last for fifty years. In this he agreed to pay the Sarmatians a subsidy as long as they stayed away from the frontier zone.

All remained quiet in the following half-century and the Iazyges got to know their Germanic neighbours, the Marcomanni and the Quadi. These people, like all the other Germanic tribes, were not nomadic pastoralists but farmers and stock-rearers. They were also proud warriors who very likely developed their cavalry skills as they mingled more and more with the Iazyges.

In AD 169 a combined force of Iazyges, Marcomanni and Quadi set out on a planned invasion of the Roman province of Pannonia, today's northern Croatia. After a tough and fiercely contested campaign, in AD 175 the invaders were decidedly beaten by the Roman emperor Marcus Aurelius, who subsequently awarded himself the title of 'Sarmaticus'. As tribute he demanded that the Iazyges supply the empire with 8000 fully equipped heavy cavalrymen. This they did. Marcus Aurelius immediately dispatched 5500 of these heavy-cavalry auxiliaries to one of the empire's hottest trouble spots: Hadrian's Wall, the barrier which separated barbarian Pictish Scotland from the wealthy Roman province of Britain.

So it was that in AD 175 a huge force of Sarmatian cavalrymen set off to cross Europe to Britain – 5500 men with their animals; maybe 15,000 tough steppe war-horses, stallions and mares with colts at their sides, to provide a breeding pool at their destination; a baggage train carrying bedding, tents, weaponry, supplies, fodder for the animals.

There is no evidence that their women accompanied them – no traces of Sarmatian jewellery, make-up, mirrors or anything of that sort in Roman forts, settlements or graveyards in Britain. But bearing in mind what proud independent women they were and the respect that their menfolk held for them, it seems most likely that they would have opted to stay on the steppes and fend for themselves. In fact they probably were not present at the scene of surrender, having stayed safely east of the Danube while their menfolk raided deep into western Europe.

Press-ganged into the Roman army as auxiliary cavalry, and riding under their own banner of the flying dragon, the Sarmatians now came under Roman command, the general in charge sporting the unusual name of Lucius Artorius Castus. Besides their prized weapons, each man carried his private possessions in his saddle bags – a personal tool-kit for repairing and replacing his weapons and armour, maybe a drinking cup, a knife, some spare clothes.

But their material possessions were not the only things these steppe warriors carried to Britain. Although the Romans chose to cast them as ignorant barbarians, they were in fact the bearers of a proud and complex culture nearly 1000 years old. These were the direct descendants of warriors who had penetrated the heart of the ancient civilizations of the Near East and ancient Egypt to the west, and taken wives, silks and treasure from the Emperors of China in the east. Their forebears were among the fiercest and most wily fighters in the world, and they had perfected the art of using their cavalry to tip the balance of power to favour whichever side they backed.

Having surveyed both the written records and the archaeological heritage relating to the first steppe nomads to come to the shores of Britain, we now have a fairly specific understanding of the invisible cultural baggage these people brought with them, as well as an accurate picture of their material goods and chattels.

These are people who not only practice but actually believe in the virtues of mobility. They understand well the economic, political and military advantages that mobility brings to them. They keep on the move on horseback and in wagons and carts. Their nomadism is not aimless (no nomads have ever just wandered aimlessly). They move from one chosen site to another, always within easy reach of sources of water, for both animals and people. We know that some of these crucial water sources are deemed to be holy places. In their lands there are also fortified settlements occupied by sedentary peasants, and a part of the nomads' movements take them to and from these fixed points.

While prowess in single combat defines personal prestige, these are also highly disciplined fighters adept at carrying out precisely defined manoeuvres such as the 'feint attack' in the frenzy of battle. They understand chains of command and adhere to their place within it.

Being on horseback is the definitive mark of social superiority, and the maintenance of this superiority depends upon being 'over-lords' of submissive populations who are either lower strata of their own ethnic group or (more commonly) subject peoples who are 'protected' by the warrior élite. The latter also require quite an array of artisans on the ground to make, repair and replace their weaponry, armour and other worldly goods as well as the luxury items so coveted by the overlords. Retaining their dominant position depends in part upon inherent birthright and membership of specific royal or noble kin groups, but it can also be 'won' by force of arms and/or marriage alliance.

This mounted élite learnt centuries before they came to Britain how to make the most from a situation where conflict was already in existence. They knew that their unique skills would almost always tip the balance of power in favour of the group they chose to ally with. Their confidence in their own abilities had led them to undertake many a quest and adventure, and I have little doubt that as the men set off for an unknown future far to the west, many of them relished the prospect.

They also knew about mystical power in battle and the use of terror. As already mentioned, they took heads, scalps, scalped beards, made capes with their victims' hair, drank blood from the skulls of their vanquished enemies. Human blood contained mystical power which passed on the essence of the victim, but it also cemented the deepest bond between blood-brothers. Magic, in the form of magic swords, also helped to secure victory. These they thrust into the ground and pulled out from it after sacrifice and blood-bathing were complete. Fire played a role in their rituals, too, and they sometimes set light to a funeral chamber before sealing it off. The dragons, which were such a favoured token, may well have breathed fire – as dragons are said to do.

Their rituals, adornments and myths all tell of the transformation of animals – of horses into deer – of snake-woman goddesses and fabulous griffins, sphinxes and dragons which adorned their bodies, clothes, furnishing and minds. We catch glimpses of these beasts in their recorded mythology, and can guess that like all great adventurers they would have spun rich tales of their derring-do long ago in far-off distant lands. As these tales passed from mouth to mouth over the generations they were doubtless embroidered into the very stuff of myth and legend, so that by the time these people reached Britain they would have had many a fine yarn to spin by the fire on a wintry wet evening on Hadrian's Wall.

We do not know exactly what those stories might have been, but is it not more than coincidence that practically every cultural feature I have just outlined is to be found in one version or another of the Arthurian canon?

CHAPTER SEVEN

The Melting Pot

IT MUST HAVE BEEN AN IMPRESSIVE SIGHT, THOSE 5500 MEN WITH THEIR thousands of horses and long baggage train, threading their way across Europe from the Hungarian plain to the shores of the Channel. Camped out every night in their tents, wagons drawn tight into defensive circles, animals corralled inside, fires burning, cauldrons bubbling, orders yelled in Latin, greetings called in Iranian, the clanking of armour and the chinking of harnesses. They probably waited a long time at the Channel – there were so many men and beasts to ferry over, and in those days the boats could only cross successfully when the winds were set right. Even the mighty Julius Caesar's ship-borne army was blown off course, at the start of the second invasion in 54 BC, and ended up having to row strenuously to the shore a long way west of the white cliffs of Dover.

The coming of the huge cavalry force must have seemed like a new invasion to the resident Britons. Caesar himself had invaded with only 4000 cavalry, but here were 1500 more than that number disembarking with all their livestock, supplies and equipment, then heading north. Word of the coming of the tall, fair horse-warriors must have spread rapidly the length and breadth of the island.

By the time of the horsemen's arrival the Romans had been in control of the richest parts of Britain for more than a hundred years. Only Cornwall, Wales and Scotland had not been successfully annexed and subdued. After a stormy first thirty years, by about AD 90 the Romans had overcome the various independent 'kingdoms' which divided the Britons. The last to fall into line were the Brigantes who controlled most of the territory from (modern) Derbyshire to the Scottish 'frontier', where Hadrian had built his wall in AD 122. Beyond this line there were several other 'tribes' who were ethnically Britons, and who were in general allied with the Romans and their Briton subjects. The most powerful of these was the Votadini. Beyond them, the tribes were consistently hostile – both to the Britons and the Romans. These were the Picts, Caledonii and Scottii (from Ireland). They not only refused Roman hegemony, they frequently raided south of the border – hence the building and manning of Hadrian's Wall to keep them out.

Although the Romans would have us believe that – with the northern threat effectively sealed off – Britain was stable, peaceful and prosperous, there is much evidence to suggest that undercurrents of unrest persisted, especially in the northern parts of the province. Also, although the Romans had assumed overall control they had left much of the British social hierarchy intact, allowing British nobles, chiefs and even 'kings' to administer their own domains. Rivalry for the favours of the Romans – as well as the traditional friction between ruling families and their allies – persisted between powerful British dynasties. The Romans never questioned their own cultural superiority, and sought to seduce the Britons with their brand of 'civilization'. Tacitus, writing of his father-in-law Agricola around AD 98, summed up the situation with glitteringly Roman cynicism:

> To induce a people hitherto scattered, uncivilised and therefore prone to fight, to grow pleasurably inured to peace and ease, Agricola gave private encouragement and official assistance to the building of temples, public squares and private mansions . . . competition to gain honour from him was as effective as compulsion . . . And so the Britons were gradually led on to the amenities that make vice agreeable – arcades, baths and sumptuous banquets. They spoke of such novelties as 'civilisation' when they were really only a feature of their enslavement.

This approach evidently worked well in the affluent south of Britain, but in the poorer, tougher north resentment at Roman occupation persisted, inflamed by the relatively low investment in 'civilization' expended by the Romans in those areas. As late as AD 155, the Brigantes had been in open revolt for three years before the Romans regained control of the north, and tensions were still running high when Marcus Aurelius defeated the Iazyges and sent them to Hadrian's Wall twenty years later. He had apparently planned to punish the Iazyges much more severely and expel them from the empire, but the situation was so pressing in Britain that he dispatched this great force of steppe warriors there instead.

The decision to send so many, so quickly, was in itself remarkable, especially as they were all cavalrymen. In normal circumstances the cavalry (known as the *ala* – 'wings') attached to a Roman legion of 5000 infantry numbered only about 120 men. In the *cohors equitata* (cavalry cohort), there were between 350 and 420 infantry mixed with 120 cavalry, but the idea of cavalry being numerically superior to infantry was anathema to the Romans in those days, except in special circumstances.

Such circumstances existed at Hadrian's Wall. By the late second century there were about 12,000 troops garrisoning the wall. This was done by manning the forts and the milecastles, which were fortified gateways set at mile intervals along the wall. This duty lay with the infantry, but they did not patrol the top of the wall on foot. Rather, their job was to control the passage of civilians through the gates in the wall and keep watch from the look-out towers at the milecastles. The cavalry's job was to patrol in front of the wall, scouting for signs of enemy raiding parties and intercepting them before they besieged the wall.

The wall itself did not prevent pedestrian raiders from slipping over, but horses could not scale it, so the only way the Picts or Caledonii could mount an effective long-range sortie was to breach one of the milecastles. The Romans had discovered that the most effective way to see off that threat was by constantly patrolling in front of the wall on horseback. When the Iazyges arrived at the wall they were clearly ordered to take over these duties – perhaps under their own officers, but under the overall control of their Roman commander, Lucius Artorius Castus.

We can assume that it took a couple of years for the cavalrymen to cross from Hungary to northern England and get settled into their new posts on the wall, in an atmosphere which was already tense, with sporadic raids and probing attacks from the tribes to the north – a regular feature of frontier life. In AD 180, things boiled over and a large force of marauders successfully breached the wall and made their way south down the eastern Roman road, Dere Street, as far as York. There they killed the Roman governor, massacred an entire legion and pillaged the town. The revolt was not fully suppressed until 184, then in 185 the army in Britain mutinied. More trouble ensued all through the last years of the second century, doubtless pitching the Iazyges cavalry (who became known as Sarmatians in Britain) into many precarious fights. They had arrived in turbulent times.

In 1994, two leading American Arthurian scholars, C. Scott Littleton and Linda Malcor, proposed that this series of events could be the key to understanding Nennius's list of Arthurian battles. Their theory is that the real Arthur was the Roman general Lucius Artorius Castus, who was charged with restoring order in the north of Britain and who had to deal with the raiders from the north. Littleton has constructed a feasible scenario based on the names of the battles supplied by Nennius, suggesting a sustained raid which struck first south, down Dere Street to York, then cut across the Pennines to the Sarmatians' rear base at Ribchester. After a battle there, the invaders were forced down to the mouths of the rivers Ribble and Douglas on the Lancastrian coast where a series of battles followed as the raiders retreated up the Douglas valley. They then crossed back over the Pennines, and were eventually driven back into Scotland and decisively beaten there by Lucius Artorius Castus and his Sarmatian cavalry.

It is a fascinating theory supported by toponymic evidence (although it occurs entirely in the wrong order) but, other than the battle at the 'city of the Legions' and the unusual name of the Roman general in charge, there is no other historical evidence to support it.

We have precious few details about the fates of the Iazyges in Britain, but we do know that their units survived in northern

Britain for at least the whole of the third century and that they remained identifiable throughout the fourth century. Their veterans retired to a settlement at the cavalry fort of Bremetennacum Veteranorum, near the modern town of Ribchester, Lancashire, which was also their rear-echelon base when on leave from the front line on the wall. A plaque now housed in the little site museum, dedicated to the god Apollo Maponus, is clearly inscribed 'from the Sarmatian Cavalry Unit'.

Most striking of all the relevant relics is a bas-relief stone carving now in the Chester City Museum. This shows a mounted Sarmatian, with pointed hat and flowing cape, brandishing a dragon windsock battle standard over his head. Some Sarmatian beads, pieces of horse bridles and other trifles, found in the forts along Hadrian's Wall, attest to the Sarmatians' continued presence, but the records do not tell us exactly what they did or what became of them. After all, to the literate Roman élite these people were little more than another bunch of useful but insignificant displaced barbarians.

Although we know little of the specifics of the Sarmatian presence in Britain, we do know a lot about the Romans' treatment of their auxiliary troops in general, both in Britain and elsewhere in the empire. This allows us to speculate about the probable cross-fertilization between Sarmatians and locals, in both body and mind. The Sarmatians were enrolled in the army as auxiliaries. Auxiliaries were generally not Roman citizens (who were entitled to join the legions, the proper army), but were mostly recruited locally. They performed different roles from the legions, especially if they were cavalry.

Trajan's column shows (Sarmatian and other) auxiliary cavalry scouting, bringing in prisoners, burning villages and doing most of the fighting. The legionaries built roads, bridges, barracks, walls, and so on, and only fought in really big battles. Although not paid as well as the legionaries, the auxiliaries did receive wages as well as being fed and housed by the army. They were expected to serve for twenty-five years. A cavalryman received the highest pay of all the auxiliaries and was, therefore, accorded high status in the local community.

As all troops were paid, their wages inevitably attracted local civilians to the remote spots where the Romans built their outposts and forts. Villages, even small towns, soon sprang up outside the forts' gates. There were shops, inns, brothels and private homes for traders and the common-law wives of serving soldiers. The forts themselves needed constant large supplies of food, drink, leather, firewood, and ceramic and metal goods, which attracted both artisans and traders to their satellite towns. By the beginning of the third century, with 5500 Sarmatians stationed in northern England, we can be pretty sure that these satellite towns and the rear-echelon veteran centres were true melting pots where the skills, talents, ideas and beliefs of the steppe peoples were mingling intimately with the local British population.

An important attribute of this mingling was Roman religious toleration. Although the Romans had their specific pantheon they enthusiastically grafted other people's gods on to their own, integrating many of the local Celtic deities into their shrines and ceremonies. They were also completely relaxed about the arrival of new cults, some of which definitely came from Asia and the East. There is, for example, a well-preserved Mythraic temple at roughly the mid-point of Hadrian's Wall.

We can be pretty certain that this religious tolerance, with its all-embracing syncretism, would have been extended to the newly arrived Sarmatians, with their belief in the divine sword as war-god, worshipped by being thrust into and withdrawn from the ground. The divine sword was such a potent and central symbol to the

Sarmatians that when a solid body of 5500 men were placed in a situation of religious tolerance amid other (Roman and British) soldiers, it seems near-certain that they would have proudly carried out their traditions of sword-worship on British soil. This, along with oral tradition, seems to me the most plausible explanation for the planting of the 'sword in the stone' motif in Britain, and it must have taken place long before it was adopted by the Arthurian cause.

I mention oral tradition because we do know that the Scythians and Sarmatians were myth-tellers, and know their ancestors under- took the sort of adventures which are the very stuff of which myths are made. We also know, from contemporary as well as historical sources, that our Celtic British cousins and ancestors were – and still are – both great story-tellers and lovers of a good tale from another's tongue.

As the Sarmatians settled down and learnt to speak the local Celtic dialect with their new womenfolk and children, it seems only natural that the great magical deeds of their own heroes, ancestors and deities would come tripping from their tongues and take seed among this new hybrid population. Bearing in mind that most Britons were illiterate, we can be confident that the act of story- telling was a very important part of everyone's lives. This notion is of course constantly reiterated in the Arthurian romances, where the king or queen invariably orders returning knights to recount their quests and adventures on their homecoming to Camelot.

In a more pragmatic way, the Sarmatians' skill with their horses would have been immediately apparent to all. Their horses were a little larger and a lot tougher than the local stock. But it was the way the Sarmatians used their animals which had already impressed the Romans, and would doubtless now – along with their elaborate bridles and the riders' attire, armour and weaponry – have drawn the attention of the local British nobility.

Most auxiliaries retained their own costume, armour and weapons, and some were certainly allowed to retain their battle standards. In fact, the Romans were so impressed by the skills of their Sarmatian auxiliary cavalry that, in the third century AD, they adopted their standard, which they called the *draconarius*, in all their cavalry regiments. This symbol became so popular that when the Emperor Constantius I made his triumphal entry into Rome after restoring order in Britain, he was reported to be surrounded by multiple hissing purple silk dragons, their tails twitching in the wind. The name has evidently stuck, as today's British army still calls its cavalrymen 'dragoons'.

The Sarmatians' arrival in Britain in AD 175 certainly exposed the local Britons to a new style of horsemanship, and a whole range of accoutrements – harnessing, clothes, armour and weapons – specially adapted to the needs of the cavalryman. That all these attributes should find expression in the Arthurian legends cannot, in my view, be treated as coincidence.

We can also be certain that almost all of the Sarmatians who survived their twenty-five-year tour of duty stayed on in Britain, and that their children, reared within sight and sound of the military, would naturally form the next generation of army recruits.

The army must have been especially keen for the Sarmatians to settle down and breed a new generation of sons who could inherit their fathers' extraordinary cavalry skills. They even provided a special incentive to encourage this process. On retirement, auxiliaries and their wives and children were given Roman citizenship and declared exempt from taxation. Citizenship meant that their sons could apply to become full members of the Roman Legions, be better paid, and be given the promise of a substantial grant of cash or land on retirement. This was Rome's ingenious stratagem for making citizenship accessible, even desirable to her former enemies, and it worked. To further discourage returns to ethnic roots, the Romans simply refused to pay any costs of repatriation to auxiliaries on retirement. So the Sarmatians stayed in England, raised new generations of cavalrymen, and passed their skills, knowledge and customs into the British mainstream.

Two other factors are important when considering the Sarmatians' integration into Roman Britain. First, they shared a common cause with the Britons in that both peoples were under the yoke of the empire. Roman chroniclers, such as Tacitus, would have us believe that they had succeeded in duping the subject barbarians into thinking it a privilege to be a part of their glorious empire, yet the evidence does not all point in that direction. Throughout the imperial era, there are references to 'trouble in Britain' – and the trouble was not always coming from north of the Roman Walls.

At the time when the Sarmatians arrived, the Brigantes, whose lands lay all around the Hadrian's Wall area, were very ambivalent towards Rome. And the Votadini, a British tribe which lived to the north-east of the wall, although nominally allied to the Romans, chose to stay clear of direct Roman control, by setting up an 'independent' statelet between Roman Britain and Pictish Scotland. The Sarmatians, charged with patrolling the 'no man's land' in front of the wall, were working in the lands of these independent Britons and doubtless mixing with them socially as well as fighting alongside them. Recalling that the continental Sarmatians had maintained a similarly ambiguous relationship with the Romans in their Hungarian homelands, it makes sense that they would have felt a strong affinity for peoples such as the Brigantes and Votadini.

Second, we should not forget that even in defeat these men considered themselves among the finest warriors alive, members of the ruling élite of their own people. For centuries they and their forebears had seen it as their right, enforceable by feats of arms, to ally with and marry into equivalent families of the people they were rubbing shoulders with, be they other nomads, Goths, Vandals, Gauls or Britons. The fact that they could win victories in single combat as well as in mass battles singled them out as special, and would certainly have aroused the respect, maybe even the awe of the local British leaders.

Just as had happened elsewhere in Asia, the Near East and eastern Europe, once a leader had seen what these warriors were capable of he would certainly make a strenuous effort to recruit them to his cause. So it seems most likely that at least the Sarmatian leaders were not simply assimilated into the local peasantry, but mixed with and intermarried with their British equals – the mounted aristocracy of the Brigantes and Votadini.

In 1999, the Scottish author Alistair Moffat argued forcefully for the infusion of Sarmatian equestrian skills and blood into the Votadini tribe – the only Britons who, living as they did outside the Roman military cloak and charged with keeping the Picts at bay, retained their military prowess throughout the Roman occupation. This all seems highly probable.

Moffat then takes up the infamous Nennius battle list and makes his own toponymically based case for the fighting of Arthur's battles on or near Scottish soil. Interestingly, he identifies several of the same locations as those that Littleton proposed, although neither knew of the other's work at the time.

Moffat also asserts that Arthur was fighting the Picts (not the Saxons as Nennius maintains), although he places his Arthur in the conventional time-zone, around AD 500. Unfortunately, once again, aside from the toponymic evidence (which also does not occur in the right order) for the battle sequence, there is no other corroboration for the existence of this Scottish Dark Age Arthur.

Even though they did not come as conquerors, the Sarmatians certainly came to Britain in impressive style and left their mark – a mark which has an unmistakably Arthurian ring about it. At the very least, we can say that they brought equestrian skills and a military style to Britain which is archetypically Arthurian. They almost certainly introduced the notion of the 'magic sword', and the custom of planting it in the ground then pulling it free would have been an important event in their ritual calendar. Having been brought up by their own women-warriors, they may also have displayed a very different, more courteous attitude to British womenfolk; at least they would not have treated them with the contempt meted out to women by the Romans.

The major influx of Sarmatians to Britain took place in the late 170s, but this did not mean that they became totally isolated and cut off up on Hadrian's Wall. In AD 196, the governor of Britain, Clodius Albinus, declared himself emperor and crossed the Channel with a sizeable fighting force to invade Gaul. To do this, he withdrew troops from the garrisons on the wall – troops which would certainly have included a powerful contingent of Sarmatian cavalry. Albinus was defeated by the legitimate emperor Severus in February 197, while, meantime back in Britain, Hadrian's Wall was once again breached by the Caledonii.

This in turn resulted in several campaigns in Britain in the early years of the third century AD, first led by Severus, then later by his sons Geta and Caracalla. These campaigns – with the Roman legionaries surely accompanied by the best of the Sarmatians stationed on the wall – drove hard north as far as what is now Edinburgh and Dundee, and forts were established there.

Severus died in AD 211 and his son Caracalla signed a treaty with the northern barbarians before securing his own position by murdering his brother Geta. Withdrawing from the new Scottish forts, the frontier was once again established along Hadrian's Wall, although the Romans still ordered their cavalry to patrol the countryside to its north and head off invaders. This volatile climate provoked an interesting reaction from the Roman overlords. In 213, a rash of inscriptions appeared on the walls of forts all over northern Britain emphasizing the army's loyalty to Caracalla, suggesting very strongly that the whiff of mutiny was once again in the air. This was just the sort of unstable political climate in which the Sarmatians excelled.

With senior Roman figures coming and going on a regular basis, opportunities certainly arose for the Sarmatians to act as guides, escorts and the like, as many of their cousins were doing in continental Europe. Although the events of AD 175 were sufficiently large-scale to have been recorded in some detail, we know that throughout the Imperial era the Romans were constantly trying to recruit cavalry auxiliaries and many Sarmatians entered the Roman armies in this capacity. It is very probable that some of these later Sarmatian mercenaries were also posted to Britain to guard Hadrian's Wall, replenishing and extending the hybrid bloodlines first established in the 170s.

Besides the magnetic 'pull' of the wealth and sophistication of the empire, there was also a series of important 'pushes' propelling the Sarmatians into Roman territory, 'pushes' which would ultimately lead to the demise of both the Sarmatians and the Romans. One of these took shape around the beginning of the second century AD. At that time, northern Europe was occupied by many 'tribes' of

Germanic-speakers. Warlike peoples, their subsistence base was much the same as the Gauls and Britons – mixed cereal farming and stock-rearing.

According to some sources, at around the end of the second century these people developed much more efficient agriculture, using animal manure to fertilize their fields and thereby greatly reducing the number of years that fields had to lie fallow between cropping. This in turn led to population growth and the impetus to expand territorially. Chief among the expansionists were the people the Romans called Goths, who occupied the poor sandy soils of northern Poland in the first two centuries AD. Lying as this land did well beyond the Roman frontier, information about the exact nature and timing of the Goths' migrations is scant, but by AD 238 they made their first attack on the Roman Empire. They struck not at the Romans' northern boundaries, but at the city of Histria at the mouth of the Danube, as by then the Goths had moved *en masse* from northern Poland all the way to the shores of the Black Sea. Over the following thirty years they established themselves firmly in the ancient Sarmatian heartlands and repeatedly crossed the Danube to raid the Roman Empire.

The Romans used the term 'Goths' to label these intruders, and it certainly seems that Germanic noble warrior families formed the core of them, but modern scholars are unanimous in pointing out that these Roman labels were blanket terms for social groups which were much more heterogeneous than the single label implies. Right from the start, the Goths were composed of several different ethnic groupings, at least one of which was the indigenous steppe nomads. In this respect, the term 'Goth' is rather similar to the term 'Scythian' – a foreign catch-all gloss which tries to label a society which was ethnically decidedly diverse.

By 271, the largest group, which the Romans called the Visigoths ('western Goths'), had set up their own kingdom and come to terms with the Sarmatians. At the same time, many other Germanic sub-groups – among them the Vandals, Ostrogoths, Suebi, Quadi – began to farm the rich black soils of what had once been Cimmeria, then Scythia, then Sarmatia. As they settled in Sarmatia there were certainly initial hostilities, but it seems the Sarmatians accepted the intrusion of these farmers, and also began to instruct them in their military skills. The Germanic peoples had not been distinguished cavalrymen prior to their arrival in Sarmatian territory, but in the following years they clearly saw the advantages offered by Sarmatian cavalry tactics, and adopted them enthusiastically.

Confident in their new-found skills, the Goths continued to raid the Roman Empire and their attacks grew bolder almost by the year. In 250 they crossed the Danube on a major raid, over-wintered on Roman soil, and in 251 defeated the Roman Legions and killed the emperor Decius. In 268, they launched a combined assault simultaneously by land and sea, their navy breaking out of the Black Sea and pillaging the Aegean for a year before being forced to withdraw back into the Black Sea.

By 282, the Sarmatians – seeing the way the wind was blowing – were joining their Germanic allies on raids into Roman Pannonia. This enraged the Romans so much that between 290 and 313 they sent eight punitive missions into Sarmatia, but, although they did a lot of damage and weakened the Sarmatians, they failed to subdue them. Cross-border raids continued throughout the fourth century, the Sarmatians sometimes attacking on their own, sometimes in alliance with one or more of their new Germanic neighbours. When not actually making incursions, they evidently busied themselves persuading the Romans to buy peace with them in return for their swearing allegiance to the Emperor.

One of Rome's finest (and most cynical) historians, Ammianus

Marcellinus, gives a detailed account of Sarmatian affairs in AD 358.
Ammianus was ethnically Greek, but served in the Roman army for
years, wrote in Latin, and saw the world from an entirely Roman
perspective:

> These peoples [Sarmatians and Quadi], whose habits are more
> suited to brigandage than to open warfare, use long spears and
> breastplates made of polished horn attached like scales to a linen
> backing . . . They cover enormous distances either in pursuit or
> flight, riding horses that are swift and tractable.

He goes on to explain that in the spring of 358, the emperor
Constantius launched a surprise strike against the Sarmatians and
quickly overpowered them. This time the emperor was in generous
mood, and, recalling that the Sarmatians had recently been through
a civil war where their 'slaves' had revolted against them, decided to
act with clemency. Ordering them to give him hostages, he decided
to molest them no further but to let them continue to live in peace
'on the grounds that they had always been dependants of Rome'. So:

> They handed over their children as pledges for the performance
> of the conditions imposed on them, and drawing their swords,
> which to them are objects of religious reverence, swore that
> they would remain loyal.

Although we have noted that the giving of hostages was not an
Arthurian custom, here is yet another clear affirmation of sacred
swords among the steppe nomads, a fundamentally Arthurian
tradition.

Despite this reported show of puppy-like submission, the Sarmatians
continued to put in raids, in 364, 374 and 378, until they were finally

defeated at the hands of the emperor Theodosus in 384. But before then a new, hugely more powerful force had begun to make ripples from the east.

From as early as the second century AD, the peoples of the steppes were once again being pushed westwards. To the east of the Sarmatians were their close cousins the Alans who also spoke Iranian and shared a common culture, although they had received less exposure to the acculturative influences of the Roman frontier, and were therefore seen by Roman observers as that much tougher and more threatening than the Sarmatians. But it was not the Alans who were doing the 'pushing' in the early centuries after Christ. Behind them, further to the east, the so-called Huns (who may be the same people the Chinese called Hsiung-Nu) were steadily encroaching on the Alans's eastern borders. This pressure continued throughout the second and third centuries, and by the fourth century they had reached the Sea of Azov, just north of the Black Sea.

We have no detailed information about the rearguard actions fought by the Alans, but we do know that by the fourth century the Huns had a new bow, considerably more powerful than the Scythian-type recurved bow, producing arrow velocities which could pierce armour. This may have been the factor which tipped the balance of war in their favour, as in other respects their tactics and skills were much the same as their Alanic neighbours.

The effect of the Hunnic advance on the Alans was threefold: some of them retreated westwards into the lands occupied by the

Sarmatians and the newly arrived Goths, Vandals and other migrant Germanic tribes. Arriving in part as refugees, partly as invaders, there were both conflicts and accommodations. Roman testimony makes it clear that the Alans maintained close links with the remaining Sarmatians around the Black Sea, and subsequent events attest to the Alans's skills in building up alliances and finding places of favour with the new Gothic kingdoms of the region. So while some Alans entered the great melting pot of eastern Europe, others retreated high into the Caucasian mountains, forming a separate enclave which has, almost incredibly, survived to the present day.

The third option open to the Alans – an option which may well have been forced upon some of them – was to join the Huns. There is clear evidence that many of them did this, some perhaps in submission, others voluntarily. We have seen repeatedly how skilled steppe nomad groups were at joining the right side at the right time, and there was little doubt which group was on the ascendant in the mid-fourth century.

It was then that the Hunnic advance reached a crescendo. From about AD 355, they moved steadily eastward, shattering and dispersing the remaining autonomous Sarmatian tribes, and in the early 370s they broke the mighty kingdom of the Ostrogoths, moving on to defeat the Visigothic kingdom of Ermanarich in AD 376. Interestingly, the few reports we have of these battles state that the Huns deployed the Alans in the vanguard of their army, leading the attacks which gave them victory.

AD 376 was a turning point in European history. As the year wore on, the Roman officers commanding the Danube frontier garrisons received more and more reports of turmoil across the border. At first they dismissed this as just more barbarian internal squabbling, then the refugees began to arrive. By the autumn of 376, there were said to have been 200,000 people begging to be allowed to cross the Danube into the safety of the Roman Empire. The Romans eventually let them in, and by so doing sowed the seeds of their own downfall.

The story of the twenty-five years of Roman history from 354 to 378 was set down in great detail by Ammianus Marcellinus. His story is magnificent because he lived through the period he recorded and was present at some of the key moments, but its weakness is that it is very much a partisan tale – a lament at the undoing of his nation. His is a quintessentially Roman view of the fall.

Ammianus begins his book 31 in the year 376. It opens with lines which Shakespeare must have read before he wrote the build-up to the Ides of March assassination in *Julius Caesar*.

> Meanwhile a rapid turn in fortune's wheel . . . Its approach was plainly foreshadowed by omens and portents. Besides many true predictions from seers and augurs, dogs howled in answer to wolves, night-birds burst into doleful shrieks, and gloomy dawns dimmed the bright lights of the morning . . .

Next, Ammianus quotes a prophetic newly unearthed Greek poem inscribed on a buried plaque:

> Then countless hordes of men from lands afar
> Shall cross fair Ister's river, lance in hand,
> And lay all Scythia and Mysia waste;

Next on Paeonia turn their mad career,
To spread there likewise nought but death and strife.

He goes on to give his views on the root cause of all these calamities, 'inflicted by the wrath of Mars':

> The people of the Huns . . . are quite abnormally savage. From the moment of birth they make deep gashes in their children's cheeks, so that when in due course hair appears its growth is checked by the wrinkled scars: as they grow older this gives them the unlovely appearance of beardless eunuchs. They have squat bodies, strong limbs and thin necks, and are so prodigiously ugly and bent that they might be two-legged animals . . .

So the very first thing Ammianus notes is absence of beards, which he links directly to eunuchs and castration, both of course Arthurian themes. His invocation of the practice of scarring babies' faces to prevent beard growth is conveniently savage, a rather novel explanation for the Mongoloid absence of beard. Their generally grotesque scarred appearance is complemented by a colourfully exotic lifestyle, tinted with just a hint of sexual deviousness:

> . . . they have no use for fire or seasoned food, but live on the roots of wild plants and the half-raw flesh of any sort of animal, which they warm a little by placing it between their thighs and the backs of their horses . . . they roam at large over mountains and forests, and are inured from the cradle to cold, hunger and thirst . . . They have no fixed abode, no home or settled manner of life, but wander like refugees with their wagons in which they live. In these their wives weave their filthy clothing, mate with their husbands, give birth to

their children and rear them to the age of puberty . . . like unreasoning beasts they are entirely at the mercy of the maddest impulses. They are totally ignorant of the distinction between right and wrong, their speech is shifty and obscure, and they are under no restraint from religion or superstition. Their greed for gold is prodigious . . .

This wild race, moving without encumbrance and consumed by a savage passion to pillage others, advanced robbing and slaughtering over the lands of their neighbours.

Ammianus evidently could not conceive of a more degenerate, sub-human race. Yet beneath the cynical surface mockery it is plain to see that the Hunnic lifestyle is pretty much identical to that of the Alans, Sarmatians and their various forebears. And when it comes to warfare, even Ammianus is forced to admit grudgingly that they are unrivalled. Having explained that due to poorly made boots (!), the Huns rarely leave the saddle, where they may even sleep at times, he says that they are not ruled by a king but:

Break through any obstacle in their path under the improvised command of their chief men.

They sometime fight by single combat, but when they join battle they advance in packs, uttering their various war-cries. Being lightly equipped and very sudden in movements they can deliberately scatter and gallop about at random, inflicting tremendous slaughter; their extreme nimbleness enables them to force a rampart or pillage an enemy's camp before one catches sight of them. At close quarters they fight without regard for their lives, and while their opponents are guarding against sword-thrusts they catch their limbs in lassos of twisted cloth which make it impossible for them to ride or walk.

—— 181 ——

Single combat, lightning cavalry strikes, slashing swords in close combat and fierce war-cries are all familiar themes. From other sources, despite Ammianus's protestations that the Huns have no religion, it transpires that they, too, hold certain objects to be sacred. In the mid-fifth century, when the Huns were at the height of their powers under Attila, the Roman diplomatic legations sent to negotiate with him usually included a Greek observer called Procus.

Procus actually met Attila and took part in some of the negotiations with him. On one of his visits, he recalls an intriguing incident when a Hunnish herdsman noticed that one of his cattle's feet was bleeding. Following the trail of blood to its source, he found a rusty old sword buried in the grass. Pulling the sword free, he took it to Attila's camp. Attila immediately declared it to be the sword of the war-god, which had been honoured by the ancestral leaders of the Hun, but had then been lost. Its sudden reappearance, Attila declared, would certainly bring him victory and make him triumphant over his enemies. He then made sure that this story was widely circulated, in his court and abroad (as Procus's recordings testify). As the news spread, it is said that several of his enemies simply refused to fight him, surrendering rather than facing the divine wrath of Attila's magic sword.

This story was freely circulated throughout the Roman Empire at a time when rumours of Attila's imminent destruction of the civilized world were rife. The year was about AD 445: that is almost exactly the date when the supposed historical figure, the British king Arthur, would have been born. There may not of course have been any direct connection between Attila's sword and the conception of Caliburn or Excalibur, but at the very least it is clear that the sword cult was so deeply imbued among the mounted warriors of the steppes that even the Mongoloid, Turkic-speaking Huns paid homage to it.

It is no great surprise, then, to find that when Ammianus turns his attention to the Alans, he reports that:

> their savage custom is to stick a naked sword in the earth and worship it as the god of war, the presiding deity of the regions over which they range.

He is altogether less scathing of the Alans than the Huns, describing them as:

> tall and handsome, with yellowish hair and frighteningly fierce eyes. They are active and nimble in the use of arms and in every way a match for the Huns, but less savage in their habits and way of life.

He notes they are great hunters and raiders, penetrating as far afield as Armenia and Media (Persia), and taking great delight in the dangers of war, greatly preferring to be killed in battle than to grow old in peace. Besides paying particular attention to the breeding of their fine horses, he points out that they are:

> all free from birth, as slavery is unknown amongst them. To this day they choose as their leaders men who have proved their worth by long experience in war.

In short, the Alans were ruled by leaders the Romans would certainly have called *Dux Bellorum* (War Lords), just as Nennius called Arthur.

I have already outlined how all these characteristics are found in the Arthurian legends, but for my argument this repetition is very important. Ammianus was writing in the fifth century AD, as was the Greek Priscus. Herodotus, the Greek historian, was writing from first-hand experience in the fifth century BC 850 years earlier. Yet the details they provide are almost identical.

We already know that the nomads' ways of life and forms of artistic and religious expression are extraordinarily resonant with the Arthurian tradition; we can now see that the means of transmission of this 'culture' (these customs and practices) must have been extraordinarily powerful. Essentially the same ideology can be found from Siberia, maybe even Manchuria, to the Danube and on to the Island of Britain.

This ideology had been adhered to, not only across thousands of miles, but also across nearly a thousand years' timespan, with little recognizable change. Furthermore, these 'cultures' were not literate, so we can safely assume (along with the fragmentary evidence we have from written observations) that the transmission of this ideology was by oral tradition.

Perhaps this point needs a little clarification: if we go to church today we perform a series of unusual actions. We sing, kneel, close our eyes and bring our hands together. We look at crosses stood upright upon ceremonial (often stone) tables. In Holy Communion we symbolically drink human blood (from a golden Grail) and eat human flesh. This would all seem very bizarre to a casual Martian observer, but if the Martian could read and we gave him a copy of the Bible he would soon figure out the rationale behind all these strange gestures in church. So, if people were sticking swords in the ground and 'worshipping' them (is this cross-like appearance also just coincidental?), making sacrifices to them and so on, and doing so over thousands of miles and a time-span of a millennium, we can be quite certain that they knew *why* they were doing this, that there was a body of mythology which provided the rationale behind their ritual behaviour.

They were certainly telling stories which bound up their magic swords with the taking of heads, sacred blood in gilded chalices, women-warrior goddesses, golden dragons, epic quests, adventures, and battles with supernatural and quasi-historical foes. But so far we have only traced one historic means of transmission of these tales from Eastern Europe to Britain: via the Iazyge/Sarmatian cavalry units stationed there.

Returning to classical history, Hunnic pressure in AD 376 had forced a mass exodus of Goths and Alans from their own territories in eastern Europe to the Danube frontier of the Roman Empire. The local commanders did not at first permit anyone to cross, referring the matter to their master, the emperor Valens. At the end of the year, Valens decided to let them in, and, according to contemporary reports, 200,000 people crossed the river into the 'safety' of the empire. The refugees were not all Goths, they were very mixed, and included Alans, Sarmatians and even some Huns who had been fighting as mercenaries for the Ostrogoths; on the other side of the river, the Huns with their Alan vanguard ransacked the vanquished Ostrogoth kingdom.

All did not go well for the refugees, however, as venal Roman officials robbed them of their riches, extorted exorbitant prices for food, and carried off little boys and women for their carnal pleasures. Consequently, war bands formed incorporating Goths, Alans and Huns who set off in various raiding parties to pillage the Imperial province of Thrace. In 377, a major component of these raiding parties, comprised mostly of Goths, was pinned down in the gullies of Mount Haemus by a Roman army. Several attempts to break out failed, so eventually a few riders slipped through the Roman lines and managed to make an alliance with a large band of Alans and Huns, promising them substantial booty if they rescued the trapped Goths. When the Romans heard of this alliance, they opted to withdraw and free the trapped Goths rather than face the onslaught of the combined Alan–Hun cavalry. The Gothic–Alan–Hun force then continued to pillage Thrace, over-wintering there.

By the spring of 377, Valens, emperor of the eastern Roman Empire, received news that his nephew Gratian had scored some significant victories over Germanic tribes to the north of the Rhine as he marched his troops towards Valens's forces for a combined assault on the tearaway barbarians in Thrace. This aroused Valens's intense jealousy and he vowed to take on the barbarians before Gratian arrived. Calling a council of war he canvassed the views of his senior officers. Many were in favour of immediate action but, according to Ammianus:

> . . . the master of cavalry, Victor, who, though a Sarmatian, was a prudent and cautious man, found much support when he recommended that Valens should wait for his colleague in the empire, since the additional strength provided by the army of Gaul would make it easier to crush the fiery insolence of the barbarians. But the fatal obstinacy of the emperor and the flattery of some of his courtiers prevailed. They urged immediate action to prevent Gratian sharing in a victory which in their opinion was already as good as won.

Next day, the forces drew together and the Roman archers opened the battle with an apparently unauthorized attack, followed by a hasty and disorganized withdrawal. This provoked a charge by the combined Gothic and Alanic cavalry which:

> Shot forward like a bolt from on high and routed with great slaughter all that they could come to grips with in their wild career.

This charge sparked off full-scale assaults on both sides. The Roman left wing pushed forward as far as the Goths' circular wagon train but received no support, buckled and 'collapsed like a broken dyke', apparently turned by the Alan cavalry.

The combined barbarian cavalry then poured in on all sides, hemming in the Roman infantry so tightly that they could not plan an orderly retreat and were forced to slog it out on the spot. By a scorchingly hot midday, the Roman line had given way completely and the survivors had fled. The Sarmatian Victor, commander of the Roman cavalry, made an attempt to rescue his embattled emperor but found that his support cavalry had mysteriously vanished (quite possibly joining the other side). Clearly taking the line that discretion was the better part of valour, he too slipped away and left Valens to be slaughtered by the Goths and Victor's erstwhile cousins, the Alans. The Huns, too, joined in the carnage, and took their share of the booty after the battle.

At least two-thirds of the Roman army was slaughtered that day, the greatest defeat the Romans had ever suffered and the beginning of the end of their empire. It had been brought down by cavalrymen trained to fight in the traditions of the warriors of the steppes. This single event set a precedent which would reverberate throughout Europe for generations to come, right down through the Dark Ages, and into the Middle Ages and the times of Arthur's chroniclers.

From 378 onwards, heavy cavalry would reign supreme on the

battlefields and at the jousts, tilts and tourneys which were the sports of the knights and kings of all Europe. No European king worth his salt would ever go into battle on foot again.

The Romans had instinctively recognized the dangers that 'lightning bolt' cavalry tactics exposed their beloved legions to, but only took half-hearted counter-measures until it was far too late. They employed many Sarmatians and Alans in high positions in their cavalry, but never acquired enough heavily armed mounted shock-troops to be able to repulse an onslaught on the scale that the combined Alans, Goths and Huns launched that day at Adrianople. They knew how strategically vital these troops were, but they had already made a further error in their long-term plans to secure their own supply of heavy cavalry.

In the fourth century, they had settled many Sarmatian troops at key strategic points throughout the empire – the Alpine passes were guarded by Sarmatian cavalry, for example. But the Romans settled these cavalrymen under the *Laeti* system, that is by making them grants of land. This meant that a substantial number of these mounted warriors had to give up their swords and saddles and take up the plough, to till their allocated land. The net result of this process was that many of the prized cavalrymen had been reduced to the status of peasants within a generation or two of their settlement, and the empire lost a key source of the skilled manpower it needed more than any other.

The situation did not improve for the Romans after 378. The

combined force of Goths, Huns and Alans continued to rampage within the empire until they were settled by treaty in the Roman province of Moesia (the Balkans) in 382, the first barbarians to be settled *en masse* within the empire. But, given insufficient land, they remained restless, their eyes searching westward towards Italy itself. The Gothic hordes were held at bay throughout most of the first decade of the fifth century by the emperor Stilicho, but he fell from power in 408. By 410 the Goths, under their very able king Alaric, stood at the gates of Rome. Accompanying them, as usual, were large contingents of Alans and some Huns. All of them took part in the sacking of the city.

It was on this momentous occasion that some events took place which are extremely pertinent to our story – events which resolve the question of *why* the name Alan or Alain is repeatedly associated with the Holy Grail. But before we go on to make that connection, we need to back-track a little to find out who the Alans really were.

CHAPTER EIGHT

The Dawn of Chivalry

Ammianus Marcellinus asserts that the Alans were the ancient Massagetae, the descendants of the fierce queen Tomyris who defeated the Persian king Cyrus and bathed his severed head in human blood. He says they inhabited the 'immense deserts' of Scythia and derived their name from the mountains there. Of their land he tells us that:

> The plains are always green and there are occasional patches of fruit trees . . . the soil is damp and there are numerous rivers.

He is also aware of the essentially heterogeneous composition of peoples labelled as Alans, commenting:

> . . . the Alans . . . extend over both parts of the earth (Asia and Europe). But, although they are widely separated and wander in their nomadic way of life over immense areas, they have in

course of time come to be known by one name and are all compendiously called Alans, because their character, their wild way of life and their weapons are the same everywhere.

An alternative derivation for the catch-all name 'Alan' states that it is derived from the word 'Aryan', which originally meant 'noble', though of course nowadays we also infer a racial stereotype from the word – a stereotype which, incidentally, fits very well the contemporary descriptions of Alans as tall and handsome blonds with frighteningly fierce blue or green eyes.

If they were indeed the direct descendants of the Massagetae then their homelands would have been to the east of the Caspian, but, as with all their predecessors, they too had been drifting westwards for centuries, and by the first century AD they were established along the river Don and on the Sea of Azov just north of the Black Sea. There were also groups of Alans living closer to the Roman frontier on the western shore of the Black Sea.

In the early decades of the first century the eastern Alans repeated the tactics of their Scythian ancestors and sent a large raiding party into Media, taking on and beating the Parthians, and then heading home with a huge haul of looted treasure as well as hostages. As Rome was hostile to the Parthians at that time, they looked on with interest at the Alan military prowess and soon persuaded them to attack other Roman enemies. But the Alans pressed on into Armenia, a Roman ally, and Cappadocia, which was an Imperial province. This obliged Hadrian to send his legate Arrian to drive them out in AD 134.

Part of Arrian's battle plan for his assault on the Alans has survived, and it reveals that the wily general was aware of the precise tactics the Alans would use. He knew that the Alans would launch repeated cavalry charges against his infantry, taking all that was hurled at them and trying to break the Roman line. Failing to do this, Arrian predicted that the Alans would appear to retreat. This was the crucial moment in the battle, as in normal circumstances the infantry would pursue their fleeing enemy, breaking ranks and fanning out to do so. Arrian insisted that this must not happen:

> . . . if, instead of giving ground against the legions the [Alan] cavalry retires to the rear after having sustained the hail of missiles and seems to prepare to turn the flanks so as to fall on the back of the army, I do not want even the light troops to make even the slightest move to spread out on the wings. *It has been learned by experience that this manoeuvre only exposes the infantry which will then be scattered easily and quickly destroyed.* [My italics]

So, by the beginning of the second century AD, the Romans already knew of the Alans's famed battle tactic – the 'feigned retreat' – a tactic they would deploy repeatedly and usually successfully for at least another 900 years.

Arrian succeeded in driving the Alans out of Cappadocia, but the Armenians had to buy them off with many rich gifts. The payment of tribute was evidently far more persuasive for the Alans's withdrawal than any fear of Roman military power. Throughout the rest of the second and third centuries, the Alans continued to probe, skirmish and raid along the frontiers, probably penetrating as far as Greece in the AD 240s.

As mentioned in the previous chapter, during these and the succeeding fourth and fifth centuries, the Alans had to contend with pressures from both the Germanic groups moving south-east and the Huns moving west, as well as the punitive missions that the Romans regularly mounted when a new emperor wanted to dazzle his subjects with triumphant victories over assorted eastern barbarians.

We have seen, too, that in most respects the Alans were very similar to their Scythian predecessors, although they did have some distinguishing features which came to play a crucial role in their fate in later centuries. Firstly, the Alans are reported not to have kept slaves. This was unusual at that time and it immediately raises the question of what they did with war captives if they did not enslave them? The answer seems to be that they absorbed prisoners into their own society by a mechanism of ritual adoption, integrating captives into their own clan structure. In a society as heterogeneous as the Alans, this seems quite feasible, and it is certainly a feature of other warrior nomad groups such as the Tuareg of the Sahara. In a sense, the Alannic 'people' were themselves the product of this process on a broader stage, where whole peoples were first conquered by 'Alans' then absorbed wholesale into the existing social structure.

Nor was the opportunity to advance within Alannic society restricted to 'insiders'. The criterion for leadership was skill and experience in combat. In this respect the Alans differed markedly from both their Germanic neighbours and the more distant Celtic Gauls and Britons. These latter groups were governed by councils of venerated elders, but the Alans scorned older men as cowardly and past their prime.

Complementing the Alans's ability to absorb outsiders was their ability to be absorbed themselves. By the fourth century AD, their territorial integrity had been shattered, with Huns and Goths dividing them into several pockets and assimilating some of them altogether. In this period there are numerous examples of Alans abandoning their native tongue, giving up being nomads and turning to farming and the like. Yet even when settled, the Alans clung to much of their heritage, particularly their equestrian skills.

This ability to befriend people, to take their side while still retaining a sense of their own distinct identity, would serve the Alans well as they rode out the period of Great Migrations all along the eastern Roman frontiers.

Alan history in the fifth century is complicated because by those times they no longer operated as a single unit, but had become fragmented into at least six groups. One group had retreated high into the mountains of the Caucasus, where they retained their independence for centuries, and where today their descendants still speak the last surviving Iranian language in Russia. Other groups clung on to their herds and continued to pasture them around the north-west corner of the Black Sea. Here they appear to have remained territorially and politically independent for much of the fifth and sixth centuries, although they probably paid homage to the Huns at the height of the latter's powers.

Shortly after the débâcle at Adrianople, the western emperor Gratian lured a considerable number of Alans into the Roman army with hefty bribes and stationed them in northern Italy. By showing such strong favour to the Alans, Gratian evidently alienated his own officers, who assassinated him. His successor, Theodosius, understood the value of these key Alan troopers and kept them well supplied. As the Goths under Alaric – supported by other Alans – probed the Italian frontiers, Theodosius repeatedly called upon the Romanized Alans to hold off the advancing Goths.

In 401, the Roman commander Stilicho placed Alan cavalry in a key position against Alaric's Goths at the Battle of Pollentia. The Romans won, but their Alans failed to capture Alaric and were suspected of collusion with the enemy (a not unreasonable theory as they were fighting fellow Alans on the Gothic side). This so incensed the Alan commander, Saul, that at the next engagement with Alaric, the Battle of Verona, he personally led a charge from the right flank into the Goths and was killed in the mêlée. His death appeared to cause his troops confusion and they seemed to retreat, but as Stilicho's infantry entered the fray the Alans rapidly re-formed and countered and defeated the enemy. The Alannic 'feigned retreat' scored once again.

The Alans in Italy continued to defend the empire until at least AD 487, and one of the Empire's most prestigious cavalry regiments was known as the *Comites Alani*. It seems that these Alans, having opted for assimilation into the Roman Empire, stuck loyally to their choice, even though the turmoil all around them must have tempted them to change sides on numerous occasions.

These loyal Alans came into direct conflict with their fellows when Alaric and the Goths moved against Rome repeatedly in the first decade of the fifth century. By 410, Rome stood undefended before them and Alaric's (mostly Christian) Visigoths and (pagan) Alans poured in. The sacking was recorded in detail by Orosius, who recalled a particular incident where a Christian Goth entered a church in search of gold and was met by an old nun who said she had an enormous cache of jewelled plate, the treasures of none other than the Apostle St Peter. The Goth, stunned by the nun's revelation, sent word of the discovery to Alaric, who immediately ordered that the treasures and the nun be brought to (St Peter's) basilica under escort.

The church where the treasure was found was on the other side of the city, so:

The gold and silver vessels were distributed, each to a different person; they were carried high above the head in plain sight, to the wonder of all beholders. The pious procession was guarded by a double line of drawn swords; Romans and barbarians in concert raised a hymn to God in public . . . From every quarter the vessels of Christ mingled with the vessels of Peter, and many pagans even joined in making profession, though not in true faith.

Although the treasures were all supposed to be transferred to the basilica, it seems not everything arrived. Furthermore, another observer, Procopius, tells us that the emerald-adorned treasures of Solomon, looted by the Romans from Jerusalem, were among other treasures to disappear from Rome in 410. This treasure contained a large golden chalice inlaid with jewels. As Alaric's troops were mostly Christian, the chief suspects for the sequestration of these super-holy relics has fallen upon the pagan Alans. As mentioned before, all the steppe nomads revered sacred cups associated with fertility and human sacrificial blood, so the 'discovery' of an important ritual vessel among their booty must have been a little like the moment when Attila 'discovered' the sacred sword of the war-god, brought to him by the cow-herd.

There is no evidence that by this date Christianity had incorporated the notion of a magical cup with powers of healing and immortality into its central dogma, although these ideas had very broad currency among the pagan Celtic, Germanic and Iranian peoples of Europe of the time. The idea that this holy cup should become lost, stolen, or at least spirited away from its proper shrine, is also untraceable prior to this period. So it does seem pretty certain that a Grail-like object did disappear at this time, and that it left Rome in the company of barbarians, at least some of whom were Alans.

The Visigoth king Alaric died shortly after the sack of Rome and was succeeded by Athaulf. In 413, he led his mixed Gothic–Alan forces out of Italy into Gaul (France), where they laid waste much of the south, annexing Narbonne, Toulouse and Bordeaux. Their advance was checked, however, at the town of Bazas, which they placed under seige in 414. It was here that one of those strange, inexplicable events took place which makes history so intriguing and perplexing.

Bazas was under the control of a Roman count by the name of Paulinus Pellaeus. Paulinus knew the Alan leader and counted him as a friend, so he came out of the siege and begged the Alans to let him and his family escape. The Alans said that would be impossible, but instead arranged to defect to the defenders' side and abandon the Visigoths. This they did, forming a blockade between the besiegers and the city walls, and precipitating the lifting of the siege. Once again the Alans – then apparently numbering only 3–4000 troops – tipped the balance of power in their own favour. Subsequently, the Roman military commander in southern Gaul harassed the Goths so hard that they fled through the Pyrenees into Spain in 415.

Why did the Alans suddenly decide to switch sides, at the height of a successful military campaign which would certainly have led to a settlement with Rome very much in the barbarians' favour? Some experts speculate that the Alans were bought off with promises of land. Others think that Pellaeus was somehow involved with the sacked treasure from Rome and shared a secret with the Alans concerning its whereabouts. It is known that in later life Pellaeus was much wealthier than he should have been, and that he inferred that he shared esoteric secrets with his Alan friends. His name, Pellaeus, is also temptingly close to the names Pellam, Pelles, Pelleas and Pellinore, all of whom play major parts in the Grail legends.

With the departure of the Visigoths, the Alans were given lands in south-west Gaul, between Toulouse and the Mediterranean, and were charged with guarding the coastal trade routes and keeping the Goths penned into Spain. But they were not given land under the *Laeti* system which they would have been required to farm themselves. This time the Alans were made 'guests' to the local Gallo-Roman landowners and given a portion of their rents.

This new approach to the settlement of warrior-barbarians was critically important. From the Roman perspective it meant that these superb mobile troops could all stay in the saddle, battle-ready, with their horses, equipment and weaponry properly maintained. For the Alans it meant that they entered the local Gallo-Roman society on a par with the wealthiest, most powerful people in the land – the local aristocracy. In a matter of a generation or two they were transformed from nomadic warrior-herders into settled land-owning aristocrats. This pattern would recur repeatedly in the following centuries, intricately entwining the destiny of the Alans with the evolution of medieval Europe.

This group of Alans remained settled in south-west Gaul and dutifully kept the Visigoths in Spain at bay for the following twenty-five years. In 440, the Alans agreed to move a little to the east and settle in the lower Rhone valley where they helped to control the local Gallic population as well as guarding some of the routes into Italy. In 457, they joined the emperor Majorian in his campaign against the Vandals in Spain, but, having beaten the Vandals, they started to raid southern Gaul and threatened northern Italy.

Eventually the Alan leader Beogar was defeated and killed at Bergamo in 464, and the remaining Alans made their way back to their old homes in the Rhone valley. After that date, this group of

Alans was effectively assimilated, but the large number of Alannic place-names, both in the Languedoc and in the Rhone valley – Allencon, Alaigne, Lansac, Alenya and many more – bear witness to their presence and influence in the fifth century.

In the 390s, other bands of Alans had been recruited into the armies of the eastern Roman empire to defend Constantinople, some of them from the ranks of the Alans roving with the Goths, others from their base area around the Black Sea. In 395, a Gothic general, serving under the Roman commander, entered Constantinople and promptly had the local commander murdered. Thereafter a power struggle emerged between the German Goths and the resident Romans and their Alan supporters. This reached a peak in 400 when the 'Roman' faction butchered the Germans, leaving the Romans in charge for the next thirty years. Most of the Alans remained loyal to the east Romans, and in 421 one particular Alan – named Ardaburius – rose to the rank of general in the east Roman army. His story highlights the extraordinary skill that the Alans deployed to achieve and maintain power despite being a tiny minority in a particularly turbulent period of history.

In 421, Ardaburius led a successful campaign against the Persians, then three years later led the East Roman army into Italy to overthrow the usurper John and install the new emperor Valentinian III. On this latter campaign, his son Aspar was second-in-command overall and commanded the cavalry. After some early setbacks the campaign was successful, and as a reward Ardaburius was made consul for the year 427. Thereafter, although Ardaburius remained a very influential figure, his son Aspar emerged as the main military figure in the eastern empire.

A quarter of a century earlier, some other Alans had been in action hundreds of miles to the north-west of Constantinople. On 31 December 406, the Rhine froze over and a large force of Vandals and Alans crossed from Germany into what is now France. The Vandals soon came under attack from the Franks, but were rescued on the brink of destruction by the Alans. Thereafter, two factions emerged among the intruders.

One faction, predominantly Alan, sought terms with the Romans and asked to be taken into the empire. The other faction, mostly Vandals but with a significant Alannic element, went on the rampage. They worked their way steadily across Gaul, where they almost certainly came into contact with the self-proclaimed emperor Constantine III who had landed there with much of the field-army from Britain. Among them would certainly have been cavalry of Sarmatian descent from northern Britain, and it is known that one of Constantine's generals, Gerontius, acquired a very loyal Alan bodyguard while in Gaul, and that the emperor created a new regiment called the *Honorians* to incorporate newly recruited bar-barian troops, Alans almost certainly among them. So there in Gaul, in 407, was another moment when steppe warriors came into direct contact with the Roman–British military.

Gerontius, with his Alan bodyguard, took the newly formed *Honorians* on his conquest of Spain, then rewarded them with land guarding the Pyrenean passes. Not surprisingly, they let their rampaging Vandal and Alan cousins pass into Spain unopposed in 409. Once in Spain, this – the original raiding group – laid waste to the countryside while the Ibero-Romans locked themselves inside their fortified towns.

After two years, the locals decided to come to terms with the raiders and made them 'guests', apportioning a share of their estates' income to their Alannic and Vandal 'protectors'. The latter then sued for peace with Rome, offering hostages against their good conduct and promising to bear arms for them if need be. But the Romans instead opted to send the Visigoths to attack the new Vandal and Alan settlements, and a long war of attrition gradually pushed the latter south until eventually, in 428, they set off in a vast flotilla of warships to invade North Africa. The invasion was immensely successful and in a short time all the Roman provinces of North Africa were under the control of Guntharic, self-proclaimed *Rex Vandalorum et Alanorum*.

This meteoric rise of a new barbarian kingdom was greeted with alarm in Constantinople where a decision was reached to dispatch Aspar (the Alan general) to North Africa to tackle the (also partly Alan) kingdom. Aspar campaigned in North Africa for three years, but failed to bring down the new kingdom. In fact, in hindsight, many experts are convinced that the Alan, Aspar, made a deal with his Alannic/Vandal cousins, as there was very little friction between the two powers for a further thirty years after Aspar's abortive campaign in North Africa.

When the Vandal/Alan king Gaiseric took Carthage in 439, the emperor Theodosius responded by ordering a huge fleet and invasion force to be assembled, but it was commanded by friends and relatives of Aspar so it spent two years milling around Sicily and accomplishing nothing before it was dispersed.

In the late 440s, Aspar's armies took a hammering at the hands of Attila's Huns but somehow Aspar retained his grip on power – so much so, in fact, that when Theodosius II died in 450, the senate in Constantinople offered him the Imperial throne. Had he accepted, he would not have been the first barbarian emperor – that honour went to Maximus in the 250s, whose mother was an Alan – but Aspar sensed that Roman xenophobia would not tolerate his appointment, and was content to see one of his junior officers, Marcian, take the purple.

This left Aspar in effective control for nearly another two decades, until Marcian died in 467 and was replaced by Leo. Although originally chosen by Aspar, Leo was determined to free himself from the Alans's control, so when rumours started circulating that the Vandal/Alan king Gaiseric was planning to invade Alexandria, Leo saw the chance to rid himself of both Aspar and the African Vandal/Alan kingdom at one stroke.

Careful not to let any of Aspar's family become involved, Leo set sail, not knowing that Leo's expedition commander, Besilicus, had been 'got at' by Aspar. The Romans were defeated and, with the Alan cause well served in both Constantinople and Africa, Leo failed to gain his independence. Obliged to let Aspar's son marry his daughter, Leo raised his new son-in-law to the rank of Caesar, but as soon as things had calmed down, he had Aspar and his sons (including his son-in-law) murdered by some eunuchs in the palace. This ruthless act earned him the nickname 'butcher', bringing to an end nearly fifty years of Alannic domination of the eastern Roman empire.

The Alans had managed this ascendancy partly because they were extremely skilled militarily and politically, and provided the services that the empire needed in those times. A further contributing factor, following the 'traditional' model of steppe nomad policy, was to intermarry as often as possible with potential allies. Many Alans were married to powerful German and Roman leaders' children, and it is even thought that Aspar had three wives – one Alan, one German and one Roman. Although the assassination of Aspar and his sons drew one chapter of Alannic history to a close, their network of intermarriages meant that Alan blood continued to influence the emerging Byzantine world.

Returning to the bitter winter at the start of AD 407, those Alans who chose not to pillage but to negotiate a place within the empire, were led by their king Goar. The Roman administrators charged with defending the northern frontier were clearly shocked by how easily it had been breached, and were therefore keen to recruit fresh barbarians to set up a new defensive line. So when Goar entered into negotiations, the response was immediately favourable. The Alans were settled in a broad band across north-west Gaul, roughly from what is now Langres, north to Verdun, then westward, north of Reims and Soissons, as far as Arras in Picardy. This swathe of settlements effectively created a secondary line of defence should the Franks and Burgundians on the banks of the Rhine fail to contain a further invasion of hostile Germans or steppe nomads.

Once again, the Alans were settled as 'guests' of the local Franco-Roman aristocracy and treated on an equal footing with them. Broadly speaking, the generous terms offered by the Romans worked, and, apart from one small episode where Goar joined up with the marauding Visigoths in an abortive attempt to set up their own puppet emperor, the Alans under Goar remained loyal defenders of the imperial *status quo*.

In 442, the Romans decided to invite Goar to expand his domains by taking over a large swathe of land around and to the north of Orleans. Their aim was to use the Alans to divide the rebellious

Bacaudae, the Bretons of Armorica, into two groups to the east and west of the Alans, and to check any attempts by the Visigoths to expand northwards. The Roman commander, Aetius, ordered the landowners of the area to co-operate with the Alans, but many refused to do so and resisted the imposition. Goar then drove out the resisters and seized all, rather than parts of, their lands. His Alans thereby became the first fully fledged barbarian landowners in Gaul, and Goar moved his capital to Orleans.

Goar was now effectively the most powerful man in Armorica, the region of France which is repeatedly cast as the heartland of the French Arthurian legends, at a time which only predates by a decade or two the presumed birth of a king or war lord called Arthur, who counted among his followers many a fine knight who came over the sea from Armorica.

In 446, the Armoricans mutinied against the empire and the Romans asked Goar to put down the rebellion. It is reported that as he set out to challenge the rebels, mounted and in full armour, he was confronted by a bishop Germanus, who begged him not to destroy the Armoricans. As Germanus already had something of a reputation as a mollifier of the fierce Alans, Goar gave him time to travel to Ravenna and ask Aetius, commander in the west, to rescind his orders and reprieve the rebels. But the reprieve never arrived, and by 450 Goar had crushed the uprising.

By that date, Goar had ruled the Alans in Gaul for forty-four years, but we must assume that at the end of the campaign his health failed him as he was rapidly replaced by a younger man, Sangiban. Following the time-honoured traditions of the Alans, there is no further mention of their great leader once he could no longer command in the field – no funeral or retirement accolades – just a silent slip into oblivion.

History, however, was rushing on and in 451 the Romans were

once again calling on the Alans to aid them in their hour of need. Attila the Hun had crossed the Rhine and his forces had easily crushed the forward defences. By the end of the year, Attila was besieging the Alan stronghold at Orleans and it was all Sangiban could do to hold on to the city in the face of the Hun onslaught.

As the Alans were reaching breaking point, the city was relieved by Aetius and a powerful force of Visigoths who drove Attila away. The relieved Alans then joined the combined Roman–Gothic force and set off in pursuit of Attila. The ensuing Battle of Chalons saved all of western Europe from Hunnic domination. Aetius placed the Alan contingent in the centre of his line, directly opposite Attila's crack cavalry. The Romans composed the right flank, occupying higher ground, while the Goths were drawn up on the left flank. As the two sides clashed, the Alans bore the full brunt of the Hunnic cavalry charges but did not buckle. The Romans repulsed the attack on their flank and as the Alans's centre ground held, the Goths turned the left flank and routed the Huns.

A year later, Attila struck again into Gaul but was repulsed. Conventionally the victory is accorded to the Visigoths, but a close inspection of the records reveals that this was once again achieved by the Alans. The chronicler Jordanes reports:

Thorismund (the Visigoth commander), having driven out the Hun band by using Alans, left for Toulouse without having lost any of his men.

These were mighty deeds indeed, the very stuff that myths are made of, taking place in the continental heartland of the Arthurian world at virtually the same time that Arthur and his knights are said to have lived and fought throughout Britain and Armorica. And the key players had wandered the steppes just fifty years before, with their tents, carts, magic swords, sacred cups and supreme mounted warrior skills. Now, with the Roman Empire collapsing around them, this landowning élite was in a position to play a major part in the moulding of the emergent medieval world.

In the century following the expulsion of the Huns, the Alans continued to dominate Armorica and in the mid-sixth century were still an identifiable group, speaking their own language, although by this date most of them had converted to Christianity. Armorican society, comprising the indigenous Breton Celtic speakers along with Romans, Alans and various Germans, was developing its own characteristics. One curious feature in this development was the crafting of the mythical ancestry of the various peoples of the region by early clerics, who may have been Alans themselves.

Although these 'genealogies' appear to date from the sixth century, two of them were recorded by Nennius in his *Historia Brittonum* in the early ninth century. He tells us that according to these ancient texts, the peopling of Europe took place in two ways. First, after the Flood, Noah's son Japhet had an heir called Alanus who was the first man to live in Europe. His three sons' progeny were all the other peoples of Europe. Second, an attempt was made to demonstrate that the Britons were originally descendants of the Trojan Brutus. He in turn was descended ultimately from Alanus, who was himself a direct descendant of Aenius and Troius. Either way, the 'genealogies' claimed hereditary seniority for the sons of Alanus, making them the original colonists of Europe. That this claim could have been made in the sixth century, and perpetrated right through to the ninth, says much of the lingering influence of the Alannic bloodlines, even as they blurred and intermingled with the other landowning aristocrats of sixth- and seventh-century Armorica.

More tangibly, from the fifth century onwards, the cavalry of Armorica began to distinguish themselves on the battlefields of

Europe. Under Alan tuition the Armoricans developed great skills in fighting from the saddle and deployed classic tactics like the 'feigned retreat' as early as the ninth century. By the twelfth century, they were said to be the finest cavalry in the world.

Alans also remained conspicuously in power. There were many bishops – and even a saint named Alan – recorded in Armorica throughout the second half of the first millennium AD, and many noble families sported the name. From at least the beginning of the tenth century, the Counts of Brittany were all called Alanus and the Normans sought out and adopted the cavalry skills of these Alannic descendants. In fact, not only did William the Conqueror claim that his Breton mother was directly descended from king Arthur, he took Alan the Red, Count of Brittany, with him to Hastings to head his cavalry.

At the battle, Count Alanus and his men put in the first 'feigned retreat', trying to draw the Saxon infantry downhill in open ranks. A little later the Normans, following the Alans's ruse, put in a second feigned retreat, the Saxons opened their ranks, the Norman-Breton cavalry wheeled and, according to witness reports, 'slew the enemy to the last man'.

Many high-ranking Armoricans, bearing the name Alan, fought with distinction at Hastings and William rewarded them well. The Fitzalan family ('fitz' is the Normanization of '*fils*', meaning 'son of', as in 'mac' in Celtic) were given extensive lands in the north of the country which they still hold today. Another Alan was made Duke of Richmond, and lesser Alans took titles and lands all over Britain. They remained in positions of power and influence throughout the medieval period in both France and England – that is, throughout the time when the Arthurian tales were being committed to parchment and vellum.

By medieval times, it is possible that the living Alans had forgotten their ancestry on the steppes, but there can be no doubt that the bearers of the name would have remained acutely aware of their spectacular and noble heritage in Europe. By then, Alans had played a key role in the fall of the Roman Empire, the defeat of the Huns, the creation of chivalry and even in the Norman victory over the Saxons at Hastings, giving them plenty to recite in front of a blazing fire in the great hall, or to recount in rhyme or saga during long winter nights.

The history of the Alans, then, attests to their geographical and cultural closeness to the fabric of the Arthurian legends, but there is still little to provide a final concrete link between the two. Yet a comparatively minor incident, generally overlooked by Arthurian and medieval scholars, provides such a link. Its source is reliable and contemporary, and its facts are as 'hard' as any we are likely to encounter in fifth-century Europe.

We saw in Chapter Three how, before the emergence of the 'glorious' king Arthur from the pen of Geoffrey of Monmouth in the early twelfth century, various clerics had reported a 'bad' king Arthur, a tyrant who was brought to heel in various ways by the superior spiritual powers of various saints – St Carannog, St Padarn and St Cadoc, among others. The story appears in its most exaggerated form in the life of St Gildas (the sixth-century cleric who never mentioned Arthur). Here Arthur is said to have killed the saint's brother while Gildas was in Ireland. Returning to Britain, Gildas forgave Arthur his sin and blessed him, prompting Arthur to receive penance from the surrounding bishops. This doubtless fanciful event is just one of several tales of the conversion or bettering of the recalcitrant tyrant king Arthur. They may not all be fanciful, however.

At the beginning of the fifth century, one of the most popular clerics in Armorica was Bishop Germanus, the man who waylaid the old Alan king Goar as he set out to crush the Armorican rebellion. Bishop Germanus had a local reputation for both holiness and military prowess, and he travelled to Britain several times during his life. Because of his martial skills, both Bede and Nennius refer to him as *Dux Bellorum*, exactly the same title Nennius accords to Arthur.

Germanus's *Vita* was written shortly after his death, in the second half of the fifth century, by a cleric known as Constantius of Lyons. That is, it was written well within living memory of the actual man it tells of, so there is a very good chance that it is historically reliable. It was also written at precisely the time when the British king Arthur is said to have ruled. As with Gildas, Constantius makes no mention of a British king Arthur. It seems almost inconceivable that two learned clerics, both writing at the end of the fifth century, should fail to mention such an important figure as the putative British Arthur, if he had indeed existed at that time. But the story of halting the Alan king Goar is recorded by Constantius, with one very important modification. Goar's name has been changed. It is 'Eothar' in Constantius's version of the incident:

Aetius . . . gave permission for Eothar, the savage king of the Alans, to subdue Armorica; Eothar, with the greed of a barbarian, was eager for the wealth of the area. So an old man (Germanus) was pitted against an idolatrous king . . . The Alans were already on the march and their armoured horsemen crowded all the roads. Nevertheless our priest took the road toward the place where he hoped to encounter the king . . .

The march was already under way when the meeting took place and thus the priest faced an armoured magnate surrounded by his followers. First the priest made requests through an interpreter. Then, as Eothar disregarded these requests, Germanus scolded him. Finally, Germanus reached out his hand, grabbed Eothar's horse's bridle, and stopped him, and with him he stopped the entire army. At this the barbarian king's anger was turned by God into admiration. Eothar was stunned by such firmness, awed by such dignity, and moved by the strength of such tenacious authority. The war gear and the commotion of arms were set aside and their place was taken by the courtesies of peaceful talks. Laying aside his arrogance, the king dismounted and entered into a discussion which ended not in the satisfaction of his desires but in satisfying the priest's requests.

These events took place in 446. By that time Goar/Eothar had led his Alannic knights through forty years of turbulent history and seen them begin to blend with the local Armorican aristocracy. A great warrior king, he had never been beaten in battle. In this incident, the veteran campaigner has the wisdom to recognize the martial fervour of Germanus and to be led away from his arrogance towards the 'courtesies of peaceful talks'. Here, then, the ferocity of the Alan martial prowess is tempered by 'courtesy', and the notion of 'chivalry' – the warrior code which embraces humility and courtly conduct – is born.

Even in his lifetime, Germanus was an immensely popular figure, which may well explain why the Alan king treated him with such courtesy. By the time Constantius wrote his life of Germanus in about 480, Germanus had already been beatified. His saint's day was set as 31 July. This meant that throughout the 'Arthurian' period, the deeds of St Germanus, tamer of the ferocious king Eothar, were broadcast from pulpits across Britain and Armorica at least once every year.

Here, at last, is an authentic figure, clearly recorded in history, a warrior-king of great standing and longevity, with the name Arthur. In action at the right time, bearing arms in the right way, and brought to the attention of the ordinary people at the right period, there is little doubt that Goar/Eothar was the real tyrant 'recalcitrant king' Arthur of the fables of the early evangelical saints. Whether this same figure would be transformed by the embrace of oral tradition into the greatest hero of the Western world we may never know, but it is surely not such a great step to go on to embellish the good deeds of the convert king into the fabulous tales of the legendary king Arthur.

There seems, however, little point in pursuing this line of argument as we simply do not have any facts, beyond those I have just outlined, to support the possibility that Eothar is the historical figure behind the legendary hero Arthur. Suffice it to say that *any* figure who managed to lead his people indomitably through four incredibly turbulent decades of the fifth century AD in a foreign land, is going to be remembered. Tales of such greatness are going to be recalled and retold for generations, especially among peoples like the Alans who treated their ancestors with such reverence.

That the Alans managed to preserve their élite positions in the emergent chivalric societies of medieval France and England, creates the possibility that the antics of their venerated ancestors would have been ingrained in folk memory and oral tradition, and might easily have provided the font from which the Arthurian tales were drawn – especially as we now know they had a fine noble ancestor named Arthur.

The history of the Alans from Adrianople (AD 378) to Hastings (AD 1066) reveals a series of key factors which, taken together, add up to a formidable argument linking their fates with the emergence of the Arthurian legends. Their extremely close encounters with divine relics, such as the treasures of St Peter and of the temple of Solomon, is directly reflected by the repeated use of their name in the Grail legends. It is not surprising that these tales, absent from the early British versions of the Arthurian canon, are quintessentially Armorican – tales which, in my view, may well have originally reflected the adventures of individuals, many of them Alans, which were only grafted on to the Arthurian canon at a comparatively late date. It has, for example, been proposed that Lancelot is in fact 'L'Alan de Lot' – an Alan from the Lot valley in south-west France, where many Alan remains have been found.

We know from a variety of sources that the Alans were sword-worshippers and that they retained their pagan customs much later than the Gauls and the majority of the Britons. We have read in earlier chapters how many of these customs are reflected in incidents found in the Arthurian canon, most of them, incidentally, first appearing in the French versions of the tales.

Lastly, the fact that the Alans deliberately kept themselves at the cutting edge of an extraordinarily convoluted period of history seems entirely in keeping with the Arthurian ethos: 'Be where the action is, don't miss it', is as good an axiom for Lancelot, Gawain, Galahad and even Arthur as you will find anywhere. That their longest-serving and greatest leader through these troubled times should be called Eothar, and that his name should be proclaimed throughout 'Arthurian' Britain and Armorica alongside a great warrior saint and *Dux Bellorum*, further endorses the profound entwining of Alan history with Arthurian romance.

The information we have gleaned about the Alans makes a reappraisal of some of the Arthurian material concerning the Grail worthwhile. In Chapter Four, I outlined the repeated association of a whole constellation of men and women with names derived from 'Alan' with the Grail. In this chapter, we have seen how there may well be an element of historical truth in this association as the Alans were heavily implicated in the removal of holy booty from Rome in AD 410.

In the Grail Quest section of the *Vulgate*, the final French collation of the entire Arthurian canon, we find the Grail being transported by Alain Le Gros to the Terre Foraine – that is, the Great Alan takes the Grail to the Foreign Land (the names themselves set the action in France, although the story later locates the Terre Foraine in southern Wales). There, Alain comes upon small people who know nothing except how to till the land. Their king, Kalafes, was maimed by leprosy. The Grail people offer to cure him if he will adopt their ways and worship the Grail. Kalafes accepts and builds a castle to house the Grail. He also offers his daughter's hand to Alain's brother Josué. The marriage takes place on the day the Grail is installed in the castle, and the couple are crowned king and queen of Terre Foraine and receive the homage of the people. Kalafes spends the wedding night in the chamber housing the Grail and comes too close to the sacred cup. A man all in flames hurls a lance at him which strikes him between the thighs, neutering him. At the same time his daughter conceives a son and heir for the new Alannic king.

This entire story seems to me to be a thinly disguised parable of the implantation of the Alans in Gaul. Moreover, the motifs and actions are specifically Alan, and *not* Celtic or Germanic. They, the nomad knights with their holy chalice, come on horseback to a land of sedentary farmers who agree to Alan overlordship. The Alans immediately marry into the ruling dynasty, displacing the ageing indigenous ruler by neutering him and forcing his abdication. No honour for the wise elders here, as one would expect in a Celtic or Germanic tale, simply his swift removal once his powers had waned, just as Goar/Eothar vanished in 450 after forty-four years leading the Alans in Gaul.

Finally, the seeds of the new hybrid, indigenous Alan dynasty are sown – and the path to integration between the two peoples ordained – with the Alans decidedly at the top table. This episode not only rings of real Alannic history, it is a perfect prescription, a role model of ideal Alan behaviour, just as all great mythology should be.

This extraordinarily precise correlation is yet another example of the consistent match we have found between the real history and culture of the steppe-dwelling Scythian/Sarmatian/Alan peoples and the legendary world of the Arthurian romances. But we are still missing one major element which would allow us to conclude with confidence that there was a real connection between these worlds.

If we could discover what the actual content of Alannic or Sarmatian mythology really was, then we could see if the Arthurian legends were derived from this source. So, what was the actual content of the Alans's own mythology? What legends did they carry with them when they left behind their central Asian heartland and rode roughshod through the annals of European history?

Nothing in the archaeological or historical records can give us anything other than a very fragmentary answer to this question. But there is a source which could shed light on this ultimate dilemma –

a source comprising both historical testimony and the words and thoughts of living people.

The group of Alans and Sarmatians who took refuge from the Huns in the fastnesses of the Carpathian mountains are still there today, having weathered out not just Attila but Genghis Khan, the Czars of Imperial Russia, the rise and fall of Soviet Communism and even the post-Soviet carnage in neighbouring statelets such as Azerbaijan and Chechnya. Today the traditional lands of the Ossetians, direct descendants of the Alans and Sarmatians, are divided between the Russian Republic and the new state of Georgia. But the people still speak their ancestral Iranian language, and still tell stories of ancient times. Their traditional tales have come to be known as the Nart Sagas, and they feature a king by the name of Batraz. And Batraz has a magic sword.

The mythology of the Ossetians was a purely oral tradition until the late nineteenth century, so we have to exercise extreme caution when comparing it to the Arthurian material which was set down hundreds of years earlier and purports to represent events which took place approximately 1500 years ago. In the same vein, the tales of Batraz's adventures, which form an important part of the Nart Sagas, are replete with supernatural characters and activities, giving the stories an other-worldly feel throughout, while the Arthurian material is placed much more directly in a pseudo-historical format, with only occasional adventures into the world of the supernatural.

Bearing these provisos in mind, there are none the less such striking parallels between the two sets of tales that we should make a brief excursion into the magical world of the Narts – ancestral humans who possessed varying degrees of supernatural power.

Batraz's tales are dominated above all by the image of the forge, the blacksmith who is making and tempering steel. The story begins with a stag hunt in which Batraz's mother's brother shoots a magnificent white hart – what an Arthurian opening. His mother is a dowdy frog by day, but turns into the most beautiful radiant woman in the world at night. This is how Batraz gets his name – the word 'batrachian' means 'pertaining to, of the order of frogs or toads', according to the *Oxford English Dictionary*. So, he is connected very directly to water through his mother's descent line. But Batraz is no ordinary frog-man, he is conceived and grows in a frog's spawn-like 'cyst'-womb which is also a blacksmith's furnace.

Shortly before Batraz is born, his mother goes to the great seer and prophetess Satana. She pronounces that if the boy were to be suckled by his mother he would be without rivals in the world, swords could not cut him nor arrows pierce him. At birth, Satana opens up the furnace-womb and sees nothing but fire. Then Batraz bursts forth from the furnace-womb and falls into the sea. His body is made entirely of steel, ordinary steel from the waist up, but special 'Damask' steel from the waist down. When his body hits the water the entire sea evaporates with a great hiss, then falls back as rain, replenishing the lost water. Batraz has received his first 'tempering'.

The child grows up under Satana, who gives him his name, 'frog-child' and he develops at phenomenal speed – after only a few weeks, he is already the size of a three-year-old. His home is under water, but then he learns how to come to the surface. There, the local children spot him, play with him, and ask Satana how they can make him come out of the water and stay with them. Satana (whose advice is always sound and whose prophecies always come true) tells them to persuade the oldest man in the village to go to the water's edge and there cut off all his hair. The hair, floating on the surface, will attract Batraz. The children should then catch Batraz and shave off all his hair to ensure that he does not dive back into the water. All this is done and duly works. (Recall, too, that Lancelot receives magical protection from the hair of a wise old man.)

Later, Satana gives the young Batraz a sword, some time before a giant with a multi-coloured beard starts molesting the local people's livestock in their mountain pastures. Batraz volunteers to go and slay the giant with the multi-coloured beard, cuts off his head and sticks it on a pole. As he returns to the Nart village, the people are at first terrified that the giant is coming, but when they realize that his head is on a pole they flock to congratulate Batraz.

In a later episode, Batraz wishes to increase his strength so he goes to visit the 'Celestial Blacksmith'. The blacksmith heats and cooks him in the furnace for a month but to no avail. So he orders Batraz to go out and slay many serpent-dragons. This he does, then burns them, producing super-powerful 'pebbles' for fuel in the furnace. Armed with this 'dragon-pebble' fuel, the Celestial Blacksmith cooks Batraz up for another month then, bringing him red-hot out of the furnace, casts him once again into the sea. Once again the entire sea evaporates, but the tempering has worked and now Batraz's entire body has become blued steel, the strongest and hardest you can produce.

Later we learn that one of the greatest treasures the Narts possess is their 'Chalice of Truth'. This chalice hovers in the air of its own accord and moves to the lips of those who speak truthfully before it, but it will not approach those who lie. In various tests, Batraz is proved honest and the chalice obeys his commands.

Another great Nart treasure was three pieces of cloth ('chivalric' banners) handed down from ancestral time. These were in essence the three cardinal rules in the Nart code of conduct. The first prescribed that to be a true Nart knight, the bearer of the cloth must be intelligent, wise and well-mannered. The second prescribed control of drunkenness and gluttony – a rule of temperance, or at least moderation. The third prescribed that the true knight should be respectful towards women at all times, especially with other people's wives, and should always be tolerant of one's own wife. Batraz qualified on all three counts and was duly awarded the three ancient pieces of cloth.

Some time after receiving these 'chivalric' banners, Batraz hears that a rival Nart, Mukara, 'Son of the Force', has come to the village demanding settlement of an ancient claim that the local people owe him women. Before anything can be done, Mukara – aided by the local water spirits – has captured and abducted all the most beautiful young women and girls to a secret underwater hiding place.

Satana tells Batraz where to find Mukara. Before Batraz challenges Mukara to single combat he has a quiet word with his horse, telling him that when he cries out the horse should kick him into the sea. Batraz and Mukara do battle, each fighting with huge force all over the mountains and plains, but making no gains. Batraz becomes so burning hot that he orders his horse to kick him into the sea. This successfully carried out, the water spirits then lure Batraz into a deep pit, where they rain huge rocks and tree trunks down on his head. But Batraz holds his magic sword above his head, and each time a rock or tree trunk hits the sword it is reduced to dust which gradually accumulates around Batraz's feet.

Stepping on to the growing mound of dust, Batraz is eventually able to climb out of the pit and disposes of both the errant water spirits and Mukara, then sets all the women and girls free.

In the closing episodes of the saga, Batraz attempts to exact vengeance on the genies and spirits who killed his father and drove his mother away by insulting her. This takes place against the background of a general breakdown of good relations between the various Nart families and culminates in a plot to kill Batraz, where the sun is called upon to deliver all the heat of a year in a single day. In the battles which ensue, Batraz is mortally wounded and instructs his followers to cast his sword into the sea. After several pretences at doing so, the sword is eventually hurled into the sea and the water roils up, turning red and boiling furiously.

This is clearly not a simple transformation of the Arthurian legends, but there is so much overlap of content that it is hard to imagine that the two traditions are unconnected. In many ways Batraz is Arthur *in extremis*, being from the start almost a sword-man, or at least an armoured being. Not only is he brought up by a divine woman underwater, but she gives him his sword, too, just as happens to Lancelot. The hair-cutting/scalping motif takes an interesting form in that it is the oldest man in the village who must give up his hair, a ritual despoilment which fits well with Alan traditions.

The killing of the giant with the multi-coloured beard is uncannily like Arthur's adventures around Mont-Saint-Michel, and it comes as little surprise to find Batraz enhancing his strength with concentrated essence of dragon. The Nart Chalice of Truth hovers in the air just like the Grail and is entirely bound up with trials of purity and honesty. In Arthur only the purest – Galahad – receives the Grail, while Batraz is rewarded for his honesty by the Nart Chalice of Truth. The code of conduct laid down on the ancient cloths has no direct parallel in the Arthurian canon, but it is fascinating in that it accords entirely with the chivalric code, even prescribing respect and reverence for women.

The incident where Batraz takes on Mukara to free the abducted damsels, using single combat and his magic sword, is so Arthurian that it requires no further comment, and the same goes for Batraz's demise, where the break-up of the local families leads to his destruction and the return of his sword to its watery female source.

In Batraz, then, we encounter a fiery hot hero whose entire being is infused with the imagery of the forge, the smithy, the white heat of the furnace and the cool tempering needed to fashion the hardest steel imaginable. The drawing of metal from stone and the forging of the hardest keenest steel was considered an esoteric magical art from the earliest times, and surrounded by mystery and awe. The making of fine swords represented the pinnacle of achievement in the smithy's arts. At least, according to these legends, the ancestors of the Ossetians reached that pinnacle in ancient times.

Consider finally the origins of the name 'Excalibur'. This is an elaboration of the word Geoffrey of Monmouth used, 'Caliburn'. This word derives from the Latin for steel, *chalybs,* which comes from a Greek word derived from the name of a famed tribe of blacksmiths, the Kalybes. The Kalybes were a sub-group of the Sarmatians who lived in the Caucasus, just where the Ossetians live today. So the name of Arthur's very own magic sword is linked directly to the greatest sword-makers of Sarmatia.

Points
East

As I researched this book I soon realized that I had set myself a difficult task. If I was to try to discover the 'true' origins of king Arthur, either as a possibly real historical figure or as portrayed in the romances, then I would need to look in some depth at four major but distinct 'worlds'. There was the indigenous Celtic British world, both before and after the Roman period, which is normally assumed to be Arthur's home world. Then there was the world of the Roman Empire, and the surrounding world of the 'barbarians' living within and along the frontiers of the Empire – the world primarily of Celtic and Germanic-speaking peoples. Joining this frontier 'barbarian' world from the third century BC was a very different 'world', that of the nomadic warriors of the steppes. Finally I needed to get a fairly good picture of medieval Britain and Europe, the times when the Arthurian legends were being written. To reach the point where I could assess the origins and relevance of specific themes and motifs in the Arthurian canon I knew I would have to get to know these worlds ethnographically, as well as historically and archaeologically. So there was a lot of meat to chew, but on the whole the source material was available, so the task was not impossible.

As we've seen I soon got the idea that the pieces missing in the Arthurian jigsaw puzzle were mostly to do with the impact of the warrior cultures of central Asia on Dark Age Europe. So this book centres on the waves of Asian nomads breaking on the shores of Roman and post-Roman Europe. But even before I started working on the book I knew that the migrant warrior cultures at the centre of the Eurasian landmass did not only move westward into Europe, they also went eastward. After all, by as early as 200 BC the emerging Chinese empire considered the barbarians who ringed their western and northern borders to be so troublesome that they started building a succession of Great Walls to keep them out. At the same time they went to extraordinary lengths to acquire their horses and equestrian skills. Just a few centuries later the need to come to terms with the nomads became paramount as the Silk Road linked Europe and China by trade for the first time. This trade route of course passed through the heartlands of the nomads of central Asia and was therefore controlled by them right up to the times of Ghengis Khan. But, as was the case with the impact of the nomads on European society, little scholarly attention has yet been paid to their impact on China and the other major cultures of the Far East. Yet some tantalising fragments suggest that this impact may well have been just as influential and far-reaching in the Far East as it was in Europe.

I've mentioned in this book that the Hsiung-Nu had penetrated China as far as Manchuria and the Ordos Bend by the last centuries BC. A sword handle has also been discovered in Korea dating from the fourth century AD which is almost identical to one manufactured in Kazakhstan at the same time. The most important single figure in the development of both Buddhism and the martial arts in China was a monk who we have a first-hand account of, dating from the sixth century AD. Known as Bodhidharma or Ta Mo in China and as Daruma in Japan, he was said to have come from the west, and had piercing blue eyes, a round face and a big bushy beard. He was said to be 'A Hon of Pos-sseur (Persia)' by the Chinese chronicler who met him. Arriving in China, he went on to found the world-famous Ch'an (Japanese: Zen) school of Buddhism and to bring the art of boxing to the Shaolin temples in China. Shaolin Temple Boxing is the origin point of all the 'hard', 'external' schools of Chinese boxing, now known internationally as *Kung Fu*. So it seems that not only Zen but one of the oldest and most complex systems of Chinese martial combat had its origins with a 'Hon' from Persia.

We know that Orthodox Christian 'Asu' (Alans) fought in the Mongol army in China. Perhaps even stranger, Brother Pelligrini, the Bishop of Zaytun in China, mentions the existence of 30,000 Orthodox Christian Alans living with their families on the coast of Fukien province, opposite the island of Taiwan in AD 1318. So far I have been unable to trace their provenance or their fate in China at such a late date.

Finally, it will perhaps by now be less of a surprise to learn that the Chinese also tell traditional tales of kings with magic swords, swords which make the dragons leap and the water roil when they are cast into rivers and lakes. The Japanese, too, tell tales of a legendary king called Yamato–Takeru who, like Arthur, has not one but two magic swords, given to him by a woman, which he uses to slay monstrous adversaries and who dies at the water's edge after ordering that his sword be handed back to the female donor.

I have long been struck by the extraordinary parallels between European chivalry and the Japanese warrior code of *Bushido*. Now I am beginning to think that this may not have actually been a coincidence. So perhaps the next thing to do is to set off eastward, in the footsteps of the nomad warriors, and see just what clues can be found out on the ground, in the vast hinterlands separating the Black Sea from the Pacific Ocean.

Bibliography

Alcock, L. 1971, *Arthur's Britain*, Penguin, Harmondsworth

Ammianus Marcellinus (trans Hamilton, W.) 1986 *The Later Roman Empire*, Penguin Classics, Harmondsworth

The Anglo-Saxon Chronicle (trans Garmonsway, G.N.) 1967, *The Anglo-Saxon Chronicle*, Everyman, London

Annales Cambriae (trans John Morris) 1980, *The Welsh Annals*, Phillimore, Chichester

Ascherson, N. 1995, *Black Sea*, Jonathan Cape, London

Ashe, G. (Ed) 1973, *The Quest for Arthur's Britain*, Paladin, London

Ashe, G. 1985, *The Discovery of King Arthur*, Doubleday, New York

Bachrach, B.S. 1973, *A History of the Alans in the West*, University of Minnesota Press, Minneapolis

Barber, E.W. 1999, *The Mummies of Urumchi*, Macmillan, London

Barber, R. 1986, *King Arthur: Hero and Legend*, Boydell Press, Suffolk

Beare, B. 1999, *Discovering King Arthur*, Quantum, London

Bede, 1955, *Ecclesiastical History of the English People*, Penguin Classics, Harmondsworth

Beowulf (trans Heaney, S.) 1999, *Beowulf*, Faber and Faber, London

Beroul, 1970, *The Romance of Tristran*, Penguin Classics, Harmondsworth

Breeze, D.J. and Dobson, B. 1976, *Hadrian's Wall*, Allen Lane, London

Cable, J. (trans) 1971, *The Death of king Arthur*, Penguin Classics, Harmondsworth

Caesar (trans Handford, S.A.) 1982, *The Conquest of Gaul*, Penguin Classics, Harmondsworth

Campbell, J. 1987, *Primitive Mythology: The Masks of God*, Penguin, Harmondsworth

Campbell, J. (Ed) 1982, *The Anglo-Saxons*, Phaidon, Oxford

Cassius Dio (trans Scott-Kilvert, I.) 1987, *The Roman History*, Penguin Classics, Harmondsworth

Cherry, J. (Ed) 1995, *Mythical Beasts*, Pomegranate Artbooks, San Francisco, in assoc with British Museum Press

Chrétien de Troyes 1991, *Arthurian Romances*, Penguin Classics, Harmondsworth

Coe, J.B. and Young, S. 1995, *The Celtic Sources for the Arthurian Legend*, Llanerch Publishers, Felinfach

di Cosmo, N. 1994, 'Ancient Inner Asian Nomads: their Economic Base and its Significance in Chinese History', *Journal of Asian Studies 53*, no.4, pp.1092–1126

Cunliffe, B. (Ed) 1994, *The Oxford Illustrated Prehistory of Europe*, Oxford University Press, Oxford and New York

Darrah, J. 1994, *Paganism in Arthurian Romance*, The Boydell Press, Woodbridge

Davis-Kimball, J. 1996, 'Tribal Interaction between the Early Iron Age Nomads of the Southern Ural Steppes, Semirechiye and Xinjiang', *Proceedings of the Bronze Age and the Iron Age Mummies of*

Eastern Central Asia, University of Pennsylvania (April)

Davis-Kimball, J. (in press), 'Sauro-Sarmatian Nomadic Women: New Gender Identities', *Journal of Indo-European Studies*

Davis-Kimball, J., Bashilov, A. & Yablonsky, L.T. (Eds.) 1995, *Nomads of the Eurasian Steppes in the Early Iron Age*, Zinat Press, Berkeley

Day, D. 1995, *The Quest for King Arthur*, Michael O'Mara Books, London

Dumezil, G. 1965, *Le Livre des Heros*, Gallimard, Paris

von Eschenbach, Wolfram (trans Hatto, A.T.) 1980, *Parzival*, Penguin Classics, Harmondsworth

Franck, I.M. & Brownstone, D.M. 1996, *To the Ends of the Earth: the Great Travel and Trade Routes of Human History*, Facts on File, Oxford

Frazer, J.G. 1970, *The Golden Bough: a Study in Magic and Religion*, Macmillan, London

Genito, B. (Ed) 1993, *The Archaeology of the Steppes*, Instituto Italiano per il Medio ed estremo Oriente, Naples

Geoffrey of Monmouth 1966, *The History of the Kings of Britain*, Penguin Classics, Harmondsworth

Gilbert, A., Wilson, A. and Blackett, B. 1998, *The Holy Kingdom*, Bantam, London

Gildas (trans Winterbottom, M.) 1978, *De Excidio Britanniae*, Phillimore, Chichester

Green, M.J. 1993, *The Legendary Past: Celtic Myths*, British Museum Press, London

Green, M.J. (Ed) 1995, *The Celtic World*, Routledge, London and New York

Green, M. 1997, *Dictionary of Celtic Myth and Legend*, Thames & Hudson, New York

Heather, P. 1996, *The Goths*, Blackwell, Oxford

Herodotus (trans de Selincourt, A.) 1996, *The Histories*, Penguin, Harmondsworth

Holmes, M. 1996, *King Arthur: a Military History*, Blandford, London

Hutchings, R.J. 1983, *The King Arthur Illustrated Guide*, Dyllansow Truran, Truro

Littleton, C.S. and Malcor, L.A. 1994, *From Scythia to Camelot*, Garland Publishing, New York and London

Mair, V. 1995, 'Prehistoric Caucasoid Corpses of the Tarim Basin', *Journal of Indo-European Studies* 23, 3–4, pp.281–307

Mair, V. 1995 (ii), 'Mummies of the Tarim Basin', *Archaeology* (March/April), pp.26–35

Mallory, J.P. 1989, *In Search of the Indo-Europeans: Language, Archaeology and Myth*, Thames & Hudson, London

Mallory, J.P. and Adams, D.Q. 1997, *Encyclopedia of Indo-European Culture*, Fitzroy Dearborn, London and Chicago

Mallory, J.P. and Mair, V.H. 2000, *The Tarim Mummies*, Thames & Hudson, London

Malory, Sir T. 1969, *Le Morte D'Arthur*, (2 vols) Penguin Classics, Harmondsworth

McDonald Institute for Archaeological Research, 2000, 'Late Prehistoric Exploitation of the Eurasian Steppe', Papers presented for the Symposium, Cambridge

Needham, J. 1959, *Science and Civilisation in China*, Vols. I–III, Cambridge University Press, Cambridge

Matarasso, P.M. (trans) 1969, *The Quest of the Holy Grail*, Penguin Classics, Harmondsworth

Moffat, A. 1999, *Arthur and the Lost Kingdoms*, Weidenfeld and Nicholson, London

Morris, J. 1995, *The Age of Arthur*, Phoenix, London

Nennius 1980, (trans John Morris) *Historia Brittonum*, Phillimore, Chichester

Nickel, H. 1975, 'The Dawn of Chivalry', *Metropolitan Museum of Art Bulletin* 32:150–2

Nickel, H. 1983, 'About Arms and Armour in the Age of Arthur', *Avalon to Camelot* 1/1:19–21

Oakeshott, R.E. 1981, *The Sword in the Age of Chivalry*, Arms and Armour Press, London and Melbourne

Phillips, G. and Keatman M. 1992, *King Arthur: the True Story*, Arrow, London

Piggott, S. 1992, *Wagon, Chariot and Carriage*, Thames & Hudson, London

Polosmak, N. 1994, 'A Mummy Unearthed from the Pastures of Heaven', *National Geographic* 186, 4, pp.80–103

Reid, H.A. 1979, *Some Aspects of Movement, Growth and Change among the Hupdu Maku Indians of Brazil*, unpublished PhD thesis, Cambridge University

Reid, H. 1988, *The Way of Harmony: a Guide to the Soft Martial Arts*, Unwin Hyman, London

Reid, H. 1999, *In Search of the Immortals*, Headline, London

Reid, H. & Croucher, M. 1983, *The Way of the Warrior*, Century, London

Renfrew, C. 1987, *Archaeology and Language*, Jonathan Cape, London

Rolle, R. 1989, *The World of the Scythians*, University of California Press, Berkeley and Los Angeles

Rudenko, S. 1970, *Frozen Tombs in Siberia: the Pazyryk Burials of Iron Age Horsemen*, Dent, London/University of California Press, Berkeley

Rudgley, R. 1998, *Lost Civilisations of the Stone Age*, Century, London

Stead, I.M., Bourke, J.B. & Brothwell, D. 1986, *Lindow Man: The Body in the Bog*, British Museum Press, London

Sulimirski, T. 1970, *The Sarmatians*, McGraw-Hill, New York

Sullivan, Sir E. (described by) 1986, *The Book of Kells*, Studio, London

Tacitus (trans Mattingly, H. & Handford, S.A.) 1970, *The Agricola and the Germania*, Penguin Classics, Harmondsworth

Taylor, T. 1966, *The Prehistory of Sex*, Bantam, London

Thompson, E.A. 1996, *The Huns*, Blackwell, Oxford

Tolstoy, N. 1985, *The Quest for Merlin*, Hamish Hamilton, London

Torday, L. 1997, *Mounted Archers: the Beginnings of Central Asian History*, The Durham Academic Press, Durham

Thubron, C. 1999, *In Siberia*, Chatto and Windus, London

White, R. (Ed) 1997, *King Arthur in Legend and History*, Dent, London

Williams, G.A. 1994, *Excalibur: the Search for Arthur*, BBC Books, London

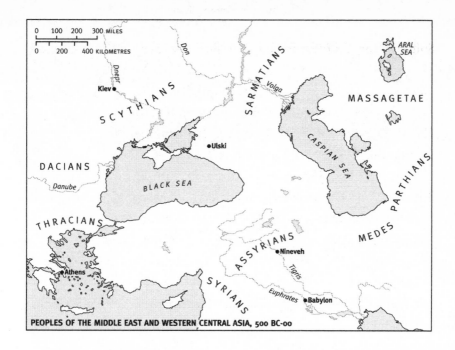

PEOPLES OF THE MIDDLE EAST AND WESTERN CENTRAL ASIA, 500 BC-00

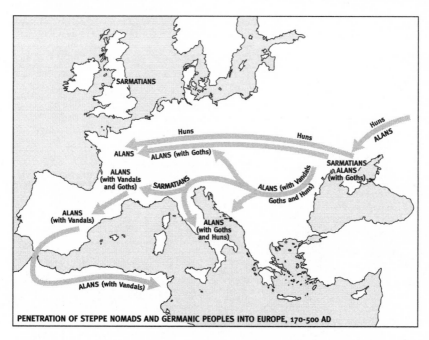

PENETRATION OF STEPPE NOMADS AND GERMANIC PEOPLES INTO EUROPE, 170-500 AD

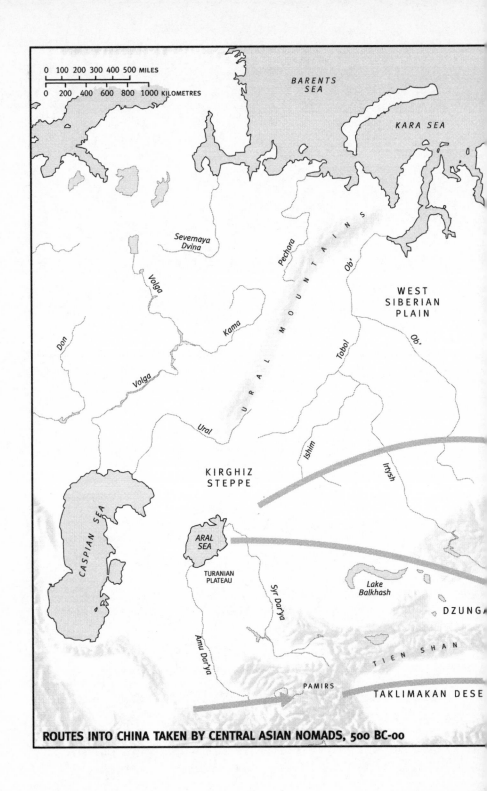

ROUTES INTO CHINA TAKEN BY CENTRAL ASIAN NOMADS, 500 BC-00

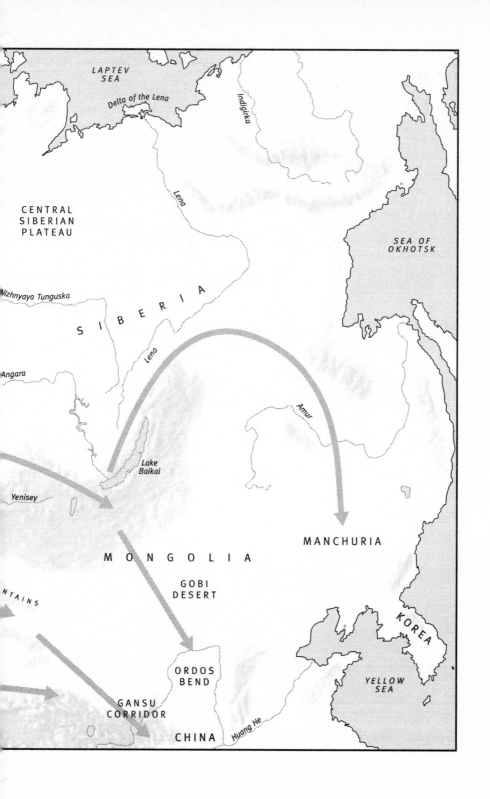

LAPTEV
SEA

Delta of the Lena

Indigirka

CENTRAL
SIBERIAN
PLATEAU

Lena

SEA OF
OKHOTSK

Nizhnyaya Tunguska

S I B E R I A

Lena

Amur

Angara

Lake
Baikal

Yenisey

MANCHURIA

M O N G O L I A

KOREA

GOBI
DESERT

NTAINS

ORDOS
BEND

YELLOW
SEA

GANSU
CORRIDOR

Huang He

CHINA

Index

archers: Hun 177; Scythian 108, 109, 139, 143-4, 151
Ardaburius 200-1
Ares, god of war 122
Arimaspians 120
Armenia 192, 193
Armorica *see* Brittany
armour 151-2
Arrian 192-3
'Arthur': meaning 81; rarity as name 74
Arthur, king 2-9, 25-6, 39, 42-3, 46-8; as 'bad' king 63, 209-10; birth 3, 67, 79, 182; and black knight 89-90, 92, 93; British battles 5, 8, 55, 57-9, 62, 70, 79-80, 83-4, 164-5; death 8-9, 70, 84, 88; dragon as symbol 81, 86, 154; foreign campaigns 80-3, 84; historical evidence 10-13, 49-74, 84; kills giant 81, 87, 220; and knightly quests 91-2; in medieval literature 75-96; *see also* Geoffrey of Monmouth; Goar (Eothar); Castus, Lucius Artorius; *Morte D'Arthur, Le*; Nennius; *Perlesvaus*; *Vulgate Cycle*
Arthurian sites 71-2
Artorius *see* Castus, Lucius Artorius
'Aryan': link with 'Alan' 192
Aspar 200-1, 202-4
Assyrians 100-1, 102, 103-4; and Scythians 107, 108, 110-11, 137
Athaulf, king 197
Attila the Hun 182, 197, 202, 206
Aurelius, Marcus 157, 163
Avalon, Isle of 8-9, 38, 70, 84, 88; Caliburn forged in 79, 86
Azov, Sea of 119, 145, 177, 192

Babylonians 102
Bacaudae 205
Badon, Mount, battle of 5, 55, 57, 58-9, 62, 70, 79-80
'barbarians' 11, 13, 14, 15-16, 122, 155
Bartatua 107, 108
Batraz 216-21

battles: Alans used in 195-6, 208; Arthur's 5, 8, 55, 57-9, 62, 70, 79-84, 164-5; defeat of Huns 206; Roman defeat 186-8, 195
Bazas 198
bear 81
beards: cloaks made of 81, 87-8, 124; Huns' lack of 180; myths of giants with 81, 87, 218, 220; Scythian 138-9, 143, 144
beasts, mythical 11, 41, 44; Sarmatians and 154, 160; Scythians and 110, 120, 137, 139, 154
Bede, the Venerable 55-6, 210
Bedevere 8-9, 60, 80, 81, 82
Belsk 117
Beogar 199
Beowulf 46
Besilicus 203
Black Sea 118, 121, 122, 134, 154, 174, 175, 192, 195
Blackett, Baram 72
blacksmith 216-17, 218, 220-1
blood: magical power of 90, 95, 123, 124, 159; and wine 124
Boadicea (Boudica) 27
boar, wild 41, 87
Bodhidharma 225
bog people 35
Bremetennacum Veteranorum 166
Brigantes 27, 162, 163, 170, 171
British Museum 108
Britons *see* Celts
Brittany (Armorica) 23, 81; Alans in 205, 206, 207-8, 210-13
Brittany, Counts of 208
Buddhism 225
Budini 114, 126
Bushido 225

Caerleon 57, 58, 70, 80
Caledonii 22, 162, 164, 172
Caliburn 79, 81, 82-3, 86, 221; *see also* Excalibur
Camden, William 71
Camelford 70

snakes and serpents 154; women associated with 91, 119, 144-5
Solomon's treasure 197
Spain 198, 199, 201-2
spears 28, 29; Ron 79-80, 86
Spoils of Annwm, The 37
stags 41, 91; carts drawn by 90, 91, 141; white hart 91, 216-17
Star Wars 1
Stilicho 188-9, 195, 196
stirrups 152
Stonehenge 18, 71
Strabo 30
sun-god 40-1
Sun Tsu 116-17
Swat Pathans 26
sword in the stone 4, 47, 76, 77-8, 86, 88, 168, 172
swords, long 151
swords, magical 47, 48, 91, 92, 124, 183; Attila and 182; in China and Japan 225; in Nart Sagas 216, 219-21; nomadic rituals (sword in ground) 122-3, 159, 167-8, 184-5; swearing on 176-7; as votive offerings 38-9, 88; *see also* Caliburn; Excalibur; sword in the stone
Syria 102; sack of temple 105

Ta Mo 225
Tacitus 19-20, 38, 162-3, 170
Tauri 114
tents 89, 90, 126, 128
Theodosius I, emperor 176, 195
Theodosius II, emperor 202
Thorpe, Lewis 66-7
Thrace 185-6
Tintagel Castle 67-9
Tomyris, queen 112-14, 191
Trajan, emperor 156
Trajan's Column 151, 156, 166
trees 37-8, 39; *see also* groves
Tribuit, river, battle of 57, 58
Tuareg 26, 194
Tudors 77, 86

Uther Pendragon 2-3, 67, 78-9, 86

Valens, emperor 185, 186, 187
Valentinian III, emperor 200
Vandals 199, 201-2
Verona, battle of 195-6
Victor (Sarmatian) 186, 187
Vikings 46
Visigoths 174-5, 178, 189, 195-6, 197-9, 202, 204, 205, 206; *see also* Goths
Vortigern 52-3, 78, 85
Votadini 162, 170, 171
votive offerings 38-9, 88
Vulgate Cycle 66, 76, 92, 93, 119, 214

Walter of Oxford 83
wasteland 89, 95
water 38-9, 45, 128-9, 158
weapons: Celtic 28, 29, 44, 151; fiery 92; as offerings 38-9; Roman 29, 153; Sarmatian 151-2, 221; Scythian 108, 109, 151; supernatural 92-3
Welsh dragon 78, 86
Welsh mythology 36, 37, 39, 40, 59, 60, 72
William of Malmesbury 62-3
William of Newburgh 66
William the Conqueror 64, 208
Wilson, Alan 72
wine: associated with blood 124
witches' hats 153
women: associated with snakes 91, 119, 144-5; and carts/wagons 90-1, 93, 113-14, 124, 126, 128; Celtic 26-7; and chivalry 11, 47; Greek attitude to 144-5; Massagetae 113; priestesses 153; Roman attitude to 12, 47, 144; Sarmatian 126-7, 145-6, 153, 157, 172; Scythian 109; supernatural 89-91, 95, 119, 144-5; and tents 89, 90, 128; warriors 14, 126-8, 144, 145, 153
written sources, medieval 43-6

Yamato-Takeru 225
Ygerna 3, 67, 79
York 79, 164, 165

Zen Buddhism 225